THE GUERRILLA CYBER DEFENDER

A concept to counter the new threats and political landscape that has changed over the last century, into a more hostile cyber enviroment where information operations by nation state actor are combined with cyber capabilities from military and intelligence agencies. The resources a nation stat can bring to bear on small to middle companies caught in the crossfire can look impossible to defend against. As nation state actor can employ by coercion, bribery or fear from the lonely boy room hacker, cyber criminals to intelligence operative embedded into academy or corporate entities. The need for cyber defenders to change is emerging. This book aims to merging the aspect and tactics of guerrilla warfare into the cyber defence space to address the inadequacies of traditional cyber defenses and counter the growing sophistication of modern threats, cybersecurity professionals must turn to a new approach: **cyber guerrilla warfare**. Inspired by the principles of guerrilla warfare in the physical world, this strategy emphasizes **agility, deception, adaptation,** and **asymmetry**—all essential qualities for defenders facing more powerful and resourceful adversaries.

TABLE OF CONTENT

The Guerrilla Cyber Defender 1

Introduction: Cyberwarfare in the Modern Age 8

    Overview of the Evolving Landscape of Cyber Threats 8

    Why Traditional Defenses Are Not Enough 11

    Introduction to the Concept of Cyber Guerrilla Warfare 13

    Conclusion: Embracing a New Cybersecurity Paradigm 16

Chapter 1: The Foundations of Modern Cyber Defense 17

Introduction 17

Understanding SDN, AI, and Access Control 18

Proactive vs. Reactive Defense 22

The Importance of Dynamic and Flexible Infrastructures................ 24

Conclusion: Building the Foundation for Modern Cyber Defense 26

Chapter 2: Guerrilla Warfare in Cyberspace 27

Introduction 27

Overview of Guerrilla Warfare Principles 28

Applying Guerrilla Tactics to Cyber Defense.................................. 31

Flexibility, Deception, and the Element of Surprise......................... 35

Conclusion: Guerrilla Tactics as a Force Multiplier in Cyber Defense 36

Chapter 3: Hit-and-Run Tactics in Cyberwarfare 36

Introduction 36

The Concept of Hit-and-Run in Traditional Guerrilla Warfare 37

How Hit-and-Run Tactics Translate into Cyberspace 38

Quick Isolation and Containment of Threats Using SDN................... 41

Examples of Real-World Hit-and-Run Tactics in Cyber Defense 43

3. Maersk NotPetya Attack (2017) 44

Conclusion: Hit-and-Run Tactics as a Cyber Defense Strategy............ 45

Chapter 4: Asymmetry: Leveraging Small, Agile Teams Against Large Threat Actors 45

Introduction 46

Understanding Asymmetry in Cyber Conflict................................... 46

How Small Teams Can Defend Against Nation-States or Organized Crime.. 48

Using Asymmetry to Identify and Exploit Adversary Weaknesses..... 50

Case Studies of Asymmetric Cyber Defense Against Advanced Persistent Threats (APTs) 53

2. TARGET DATA BREACH (2013) 54
3. CLOUDHOPPER ATTACKS (2014–2017) 54
    Conclusion: Asymmetry as a Force Multiplier for Small Teams 55
Chapter 5: Cyber Ambush: Setting Traps and Luring Attackers 55
    Introduction 56
    The Art of Ambush in Guerrilla Warfare 56
    Setting Up Cyber Ambushes: Honeypots, Honeynets, and Decoys ... 58
    Dynamic Network Segmentation and Traffic Rerouting to Trap Attackers 60
    Leveraging SDN and AI for Real-Time Ambush Tactics 62
    Psychological Impact of Ambush Tactics on Attackers 64
    Conclusion: Cyber Ambush as a Strategic Tool 65
Chapter 6: Cyber Deception and Misinformation as a Strategic Defense . 66
    Introduction 66
    The Role of Deception in Traditional Guerrilla Warfare 67
    How Misinformation and Deception Disorient Attackers 68
    Creating Fake Systems and Data to Mislead Adversaries 70
    AI's Role in Deploying and Managing Deceptive Systems 73
    Case Studies on plausible Cyber Deception Operations 75
    Conclusion: Cyber Deception as a Strategic Defense 76
Chapter 7: Proactive Threat Hunting and Intelligence Sharing 77
    Introduction 77
    The Need for Proactive Defense 77
    AI's Role in Real-Time Threat Detection and Analysis 80
    Using SDN for Dynamic Threat Mitigation 82
    Collaborating with Allies and Sharing Intelligence for Mutual Defense 84

Conclusion: The Power of Proactive Defense and Intelligence Sharing 87

Chapter 8: Zero Trust Architecture and Dynamic Access Control 88

Introduction 88

The Zero Trust Philosophy and Why It's Critical 89

Implementing AI-Driven Continuous Authentication 91

Using SDN to Enforce Micro-Segmentation and Limit Lateral Movement 93

Adopting Guerrilla-Style Ambush Tactics Through Network Segmentation 95

Conclusion: Zero Trust Architecture and Dynamic Access Control as the Future of Cyber Defense 97

Chapter 9: Resilient Infrastructure and Redundancy in a Dynamic Environment 97

Introduction 98

Building a Resilient Network Architecture 98

Using SDN for Rapid Reconfiguration and Traffic Rerouting 101

The Role of AI in Automated Backup and Recovery Processes 103

Mobility as a Defensive Strategy: Hit-and-Run Tactics for Data and Services 105

Conclusion: Building Resilience in a Dynamic Cyber Environment .. 107

Chapter 10: Psyops Cyber Deception and the Art of the Ambush 108

Introduction 108

Building a Resilient Network Architecture 109

Using SDN for Rapid Reconfiguration and Traffic Rerouting 110

Psyops Tactics in Cyberwarfare 112

Psyops in Access Control Management to Deceive 114

The Role of AI in Automated Backup and Recovery Processes 115

Mobility as a Defensive Strategy: Hit-and-Run Tactics for Data and Services 117

Conclusion: The Power of Cyber Deception and Psyops in Cyber Defense 119

Chapter 11: Offensive Cyber Capabilities and Preemptive Strikes 119

Introduction 119

Offensive Cyber Operations as a Strategic Tool for Defense 120

Preemptive Strikes: When to Engage in Hack-Back Tactics 122

Exploiting Weaknesses in Adversary Infrastructures 124

Legal and Ethical Considerations in Offensive Cyber Tactics 126

Conclusion: Offensive Cyber Capabilities in Modern Defense Strategies 127

Chapter 12: Securing AI Models from Adversarial Attacks 128

Introduction 128

Understanding the Vulnerabilities of AI Models 129

Adversarial Machine Learning Attacks: How They Work and How They Are Evolving 131

Defense Strategies Against Adversarial Attacks 134

Continuous Monitoring and Reinforcement Learning for AI Security 136

Conclusion: Securing AI in an Adversarial World 138

Chapter 13: AI Governance and Ethical Considerations in Cyber Defense 138

Introduction 139

The Importance of Ethical AI in Cybersecurity 140

Establishing AI Governance Frameworks to Mitigate Risks 142

Preventing Bias and Ensuring Transparency in AI-Driven Defense Systems 144

Balancing AI Autonomy with Human Oversight in Critical Systems . 146

Conclusion: The Path Forward for Ethical AI in Cyber Defense 148

Chapter 14: AI Robustness and Resilience in a Cyberwarfare Context 149

Introduction 149

Building Robust AI Models That Can Withstand Attacks 149

Enhancing Resilience Through Redundancy and Diversity in AI Systems 152

Testing AI Models Against Adversarial Threats: Simulation and Training Environments 154

The Role of AI in Detecting and Countering AI-Based Attacks 156

Conclusion: Building AI Robustness and Resilience in Cyberwarfare 158

Chapter 15: Cybersecurity Automation and AI-Driven Optimization 159

Introduction 159

The Need for Speed: How AI Can Automate Defense Actions 160

Using AI for Predictive Analytics and Proactive Defense Measures 162

Automated Incident Response Through SDN 164

How to Overwhelm Attackers with Guerrilla-Style Attrition Warfare 165

Conclusion: AI-Driven Automation and Proactive Defense in Cybersecurity 167

Chapter 16: Collaboration with National Cybersecurity Agencies and Allies 168

Introduction 168

The Power of Partnerships in Cyber Defense 169

Public-Private Sector Collaboration for Stronger Defense 171

Cyber Defense Alliances: Decentralized Command Structures and Unified Goals 173

NCSA Across the Globe and How to Build Interaction with Them ... 175

How AI, SDN, and AI Access Control Enhance Global Defense Strategies 177

Conclusion: The Future of Cyber Defense Collaboration 179

CHAPTER 17: The Playbook In Action: Real-world Applications 179

    Introduction 179

    Case Studies: Verified Organizations Applying AI, SDN, And Cyber Tactics 180

    Examples Of SDN And AI Integration For Dynamic Defense 183

    Conclusion: Applying The Playbook For Dynamic And Proactive Defense 185

Chapter 18: Blockchain in Cybersecurity Based on Guerrilla Tactics 185

    Introduction 185

    Blockchain for Secure Data Transmission 186

    Decentralized Identity Management and Authentication 188

    Blockchain's Role in Protecting IoT Devices 190

    Use Cases: Supply Chain Security and Financial Transactions 192

    Guerrilla Tactics with Blockchain: Decentralizing Cyber Defense 193

    Conclusion: Leveraging Blockchain for Cyber Guerrilla Warfare 195

Chapter 19: Quantum Computing: A Double-Edged Sword 195

    Introduction 196

    Quantum Computing and Its Threat to Cryptography 196

    Post-Quantum Cryptography: The Next Frontier in Defense 198

    Quantum-Assisted Cyber Defense: Potential Benefits 200

    Quantum-Resistant Algorithms for Cybersecurity 202

    Future Use of Quantum in Guerrilla Cyber Defense 203

    Conclusion: Navigating the Quantum Frontier in Cyber Defense 205

Chapter 20: Emerging Technologies: Integrating the Future into Cyber Defense 206

    Introduction 206

    Predictive Analytics and Proactive Cybersecurity Strategies 207

Cybersecurity Implications of 5G Networks and IoT Devices...........209

Cloud Security: Leveraging AI and Blockchain for Enhanced Protection 211

The Role of Autonomous Systems in Cyber Warfare.......................213

Conclusion: The Future of Cyber Defense Through Emerging Technologies 216

Chapter 21: Preparing for the Future: Next-Generation Cyber Defense.216

Introduction 216

How Emerging Technologies Like Quantum Computing and IoT Will Impact Cyber Defense...217

Evolving Guerrilla Tactics for New Threats 220

The Future Role of AI, SDN, and Automation in Cyber Warfare 222

Continuous Adaptation: Staying Ahead of Attackers in an Ever-Changing Environment...225

Conclusion: Preparing for the Future of Cyber Defense 227

Conclusion: The Guerrilla Defender's Path 227

Introduction 227

Key Takeaways for Implementing Guerrilla Tactics in Cyber Defense 228

How to Build an Adaptive, Agile, and Resilient Cyber Defense Strategy..231

The Importance of Staying Proactive and Unpredictable 233

Conclusion: Embracing the Guerrilla Defender's Path....................235

INTRODUCTION: CYBERWARFARE IN THE MODERN AGE

Overview of the Evolving Landscape of Cyber Threats

The digital revolution has brought about a profound transformation in how individuals, businesses, and governments interact with the world. The rise of the **internet, cloud computing, and connected devices** has led to unprecedented levels of convenience, communication, and productivity. However, this interconnected digital landscape also comes with significant vulnerabilities. **Cyberspace has become a battlefield** where attacks can occur at lightning speed, and the consequences of breaches can ripple across the globe, affecting millions.

In the early days of the internet, cyberattacks were primarily the work of lone hackers or small groups of enthusiasts who were testing the limits of systems. These attacks were often **unsophisticated**, opportunistic, and carried out for personal gain, curiosity, or a desire for notoriety. As digital infrastructures grew more complex, so too did the threats. Today, we face a radically different threat landscape, with **nation-states, organized crime syndicates**, and **hacktivists** engaging in highly coordinated and sophisticated cyber operations.

THE RISE OF ADVANCED PERSISTENT THREATS (APTS)

One of the most significant changes in the modern cyber threat landscape is the rise of **Advanced Persistent Threats (APTs)**. These are typically state-sponsored cyberattacks, characterized by their stealth, patience, and persistence. APT groups, often linked to national intelligence or military agencies, infiltrate networks with the goal of remaining undetected for long periods while collecting intelligence, sabotaging critical systems, or exfiltrating sensitive data.

- **APTs** can target a wide range of industries, from **energy** and **telecommunications** to **finance** and **government**, with objectives that range from **espionage** and **disruption** to **economic theft** and **sabotage**.

- Well-known APT groups, such as **APT28** (Fancy Bear), **APT29** (Cozy Bear), and **Lazarus Group**, have demonstrated their ability to carry out complex, targeted attacks with the resources and backing of nation-states.

APTs are highly effective because they are **difficult to detect** and **even harder to remove**. These attackers often spend months or years inside their target's network, collecting data, moving laterally across systems, and patiently waiting for the right moment to strike. Once inside, they often use legitimate tools and processes to avoid detection, blending in with normal network traffic.

THE PROLIFERATION OF RANSOMWARE AND CYBERCRIME-AS-A-SERVICE

Another major trend in the evolving threat landscape is the **rise of cybercriminal syndicates**, many of which operate in ways that mimic legitimate businesses. These criminal organizations are often responsible for the proliferation of **ransomware**, which has emerged as one of the most pervasive and damaging forms of cyberattack in recent years.

- **Ransomware attacks** involve encrypting an organization's data and demanding payment—usually in cryptocurrency—in exchange for the decryption keys. The sophistication of ransomware has increased dramatically, with modern variants capable of not only encrypting data but also exfiltrating it, allowing attackers to **double extort** victims by threatening to release sensitive data publicly if the ransom is not paid.
- In addition to **ransomware-as-a-service (RaaS)** models, cybercriminal groups now offer **cybercrime-as-a-service (CaaS)**, where criminals lease out their expertise, tools, and resources to others in exchange for a share of the profits. This has lowered the barrier to entry for aspiring cybercriminals, resulting in a massive increase in the volume of attacks.

Nation-State Cyberwarfare and Geopolitical Conflict

As the lines between physical warfare and cyberwarfare blur, **nation-state cyberattacks** have become tools for achieving geopolitical objectives. Governments are increasingly using cyber capabilities to project power, influence elections, destabilize adversaries, and gather intelligence. Unlike traditional warfare, which is subject to internationally recognized laws and rules of engagement, cyberwarfare exists in a **legal gray area**, allowing states to conduct covert operations with **limited attribution**.

- **Election interference**, such as that seen in the 2016 U.S. Presidential election, is one form of cyberwarfare that seeks to undermine public trust in democratic institutions.
- **Industrial sabotage** is another tactic employed by nation-states. For example, **Stuxnet**, a highly sophisticated worm developed by the U.S. and Israel, was used to target Iran's nuclear program, setting a new precedent for using cyberattacks to cripple physical infrastructure.

As state-sponsored cyberattacks become more common and sophisticated, the nature of these threats requires defenders to adopt new, more agile approaches to defense.

Why Traditional Defenses Are Not Enough

In the face of this ever-evolving threat landscape, it has become clear that **traditional cybersecurity defenses**, such as **firewalls**, **intrusion detection systems (IDS)**, and **antivirus software**, are no longer sufficient. These defenses were designed for an era when networks were relatively static, attackers were less sophisticated, and most threats could be mitigated by creating strong perimeters around sensitive data. However, today's threats easily bypass these static, perimeter-focused defenses.

THE FAILURE OF PERIMETER-BASED SECURITY

For decades, the dominant security paradigm was based on the idea of protecting the **network perimeter**—the boundary between an organization's internal network and the external internet. Firewalls and IDS systems were placed at the network's edge to filter traffic and detect known malicious patterns. However, this **perimeter-based model** is inherently flawed in modern environments for several reasons:

- **Complex and Distributed Networks**: The rise of **cloud computing, remote work, mobile devices,** and **Internet of Things (IoT)** has blurred the lines of what constitutes the network perimeter. Users now access sensitive data from multiple devices, locations, and networks, making it impossible to maintain a clear boundary between trusted and untrusted environments.
- **Sophisticated Attack Techniques**: Modern attackers often use **multi-stage attacks, supply chain compromises,** or **social engineering** to bypass perimeter defenses. Techniques such as **phishing** can easily trick employees into providing credentials or downloading malware, giving attackers direct access to internal systems without ever touching the perimeter.
- **Insider Threats**: The perimeter-based model assumes that everything inside the network is trustworthy. However, **insider threats**—whether malicious or accidental—can cause significant damage. Once inside the network, an attacker or compromised user often has broad access to critical systems and data.

STATIC DEFENSES AGAINST ADAPTIVE THREATS

The rapid evolution of cyber threats has exposed the limitations of static defenses like **antivirus software** and **signature-based detection**. Traditional security tools rely on predefined **signatures** or **patterns** of known attacks, making them ineffective against **zero-day** exploits, **advanced persistent threats**, and **fileless malware**, which do not match existing signatures.

- **Zero-day vulnerabilities** are security flaws that are unknown to the vendor and for which no patch exists. Attackers who exploit these vulnerabilities can bypass traditional defenses because there are no predefined rules or signatures to detect the threat.
- **Fileless attacks** use legitimate system tools (such as PowerShell or WMI) to carry out malicious activities without writing anything to disk, making them much harder to detect through traditional means.

Static defenses can only react to known threats, and even then, they are often too slow to respond. By the time a breach is detected, the attacker may have already achieved their objectives, leaving defenders scrambling to mitigate the damage.

THE ALERT OVERLOAD PROBLEM

Another significant challenge with traditional defenses is the overwhelming number of **false positives** they generate. Security teams are often inundated with alerts from various security tools, many of which turn out to be benign. This **alert fatigue** can make it difficult for defenders to focus on real threats, leaving organizations vulnerable to attacks that slip through the cracks.

As attackers grow more sophisticated and stealthy, traditional defenses can no longer keep up with the complexity and speed of modern cyberattacks. To defend against today's threats, organizations must embrace a new paradigm—one that is **dynamic, flexible,** and **proactive.**

Introduction to the Concept of Cyber Guerrilla Warfare

To address the inadequacies of traditional defenses and counter the growing sophistication of modern threats, cybersecurity professionals must turn to a new approach: **cyber guerrilla warfare**. Inspired by the principles of guerrilla warfare in the physical world, this strategy emphasizes **agility, deception, adaptation,** and **asymmetry**—all essential qualities for defenders facing more powerful and resourceful adversaries.

What is Guerrilla Warfare?

Guerrilla warfare is a form of irregular warfare where small, mobile groups use **hit-and-run tactics, ambushes,** and **deception** to outmaneuver a larger, better-equipped adversary. It is typically employed by forces who lack the resources for a direct confrontation but compensate for this by using their **knowledge of the terrain, adaptability,** and **surprise** to their advantage. Key principles of guerrilla warfare include:

- **Avoiding direct confrontation**: Guerrilla forces rarely engage in head-to-head battles with stronger opponents. Instead, they target the enemy's weak points, launching quick, unexpected strikes before disappearing into the environment.
- **Deception and misinformation**: Guerrilla fighters often use deception to confuse and demoralize the enemy, employing decoys, false trails, and misinformation to mislead their adversaries.
- **Asymmetric tactics**: Rather than relying on brute force, guerrilla warfare seeks to exploit the vulnerabilities of a more powerful adversary. This often involves targeting supply lines, communication channels, or morale, using small, flexible units that are difficult to track.

APPLYING GUERRILLA TACTICS TO CYBER DEFENSE

In the context of cyber defense, **guerrilla-style tactics** offer a way for defenders to counter sophisticated attackers by adopting strategies that are **unpredictable, proactive,** and **designed to disrupt** the attacker's plans. Cyber guerrilla warfare emphasizes **agility, dynamic responses,** and **deception** to keep attackers off balance and waste their time and resources. Key elements of cyber guerrilla warfare include:

- **Proactive Defense**: Traditional defenses are reactive, meaning they only engage once an attack has occurred. In contrast, guerrilla-style defense is **proactive**, actively seeking out threats before they materialize. This can involve **threat hunting, predictive analytics,** and **continuous monitoring** to detect and disrupt attackers early in their operations.
- **Deception and Misdirection**: Just as guerrilla fighters use decoys and misinformation, cyber defenders can employ **cyber deception tactics** to confuse attackers. **Honeypots, honeynets,** and **decoy systems** can lure attackers into false environments, diverting them from critical assets and gathering intelligence on their techniques.
- **Hit-and-Run Tactics**: In guerrilla warfare, fighters strike quickly and retreat before the enemy can mount a response. Similarly, cyber defenders can use **hit-and-run containment tactics**, isolating compromised systems and **cutting off communication** with the attacker before they can gain a strong foothold.
- **Dynamic and Flexible Defenses**: Guerrilla forces never stay in one place for long, constantly changing positions to avoid detection. In cyber defense, this principle translates into **dynamic defenses** that are constantly shifting and evolving. **Software Defined Networking (SDN)** and **AI-driven automation** allow defenders to rapidly reconfigure network segments, adjust access controls, and reroute traffic in

response to threats, making it harder for attackers to map and exploit the environment.

ASYMMETRIC RESPONSE TO STRONGER ADVERSARIES

In modern cybersecurity, attackers often have the advantage of surprise, superior resources, and time. Nation-state actors, for example, can mobilize large teams of skilled attackers, armed with cutting-edge tools, to infiltrate and sabotage critical systems. In such situations, defenders must adopt **asymmetric strategies**—ones that exploit the attacker's weaknesses, rather than confronting them directly.

- **Targeting Attack Infrastructure**: Just as guerrilla fighters attack supply lines, cyber defenders can target the infrastructure attackers rely on, such as **command-and-control (C2) servers** and **malware distribution channels**. By **disrupting or neutralizing these critical components**, defenders can undermine the attacker's ability to sustain an attack.
- **Exploiting Attacker Mistakes**: Guerrilla fighters exploit the complacency or overconfidence of their adversaries. In cyber defense, this can involve using **honeypots** to bait attackers into revealing their tools and methods, which can then be used to develop countermeasures.

By adopting **cyber guerrilla warfare tactics**, defenders can level the playing field, turning the unpredictability, speed, and flexibility of modern attackers against them. This approach represents a significant shift in how cyber defense is conducted, moving away from passive, perimeter-based security toward **active, fluid, and resilient defenses** that can outmaneuver even the most well-resourced adversaries.

Conclusion: Embracing a New Cybersecurity Paradigm

The modern era of cyberwarfare requires a radical departure from traditional defense models. Attackers, whether nation-states or cybercriminal syndicates, are increasingly sophisticated, well-funded, and persistent. In this environment, static, reactive defenses are no longer adequate. Defenders must embrace the principles of **cyber guerrilla warfare**—leveraging **flexibility, proactivity, deception**, and **dynamic response** to outwit their adversaries.

By adopting this guerrilla mindset and integrating cutting-edge technologies like **SDN** and **AI**, organizations can build cyber defenses that are not only capable of withstanding attacks but also **actively disrupt and neutralize** threats before they cause significant damage. This book will guide you through the strategies, tactics, and technologies that form the foundation of this new approach to cyber defense.

In the following chapters, we will explore how to apply these concepts in practice, helping you build a **resilient, adaptive, and proactive defense strategy** that can protect your organization in the modern age of cyberwarfare.

CHAPTER 1: THE FOUNDATIONS OF MODERN CYBER DEFENSE

Introduction

In the modern age of cybersecurity, static defense mechanisms, perimeter-based protections, and reactive incident responses are no longer sufficient to counter the ever-evolving landscape of sophisticated threats. As cyberattacks grow in complexity, defenders must adopt a more agile, flexible, and proactive approach to safeguard their systems and data. At the heart of this modern cyber defense strategy lie several key technologies and methodologies: **Software Defined Networking (SDN), Artificial Intelligence (AI),** and **Access Control Systems**. These tools, when combined with proactive defense strategies and dynamic infrastructures, allow defenders to stay ahead of attackers by **predicting, mitigating,** and **neutralizing threats** before they cause significant damage.

In this chapter, we will explore the essential elements that form the foundation of modern cyber defense, offering insights into how **SDN, AI,** and **Access Control** systems work together to create a **proactive, responsive,** and **adaptive defense**. We will also examine the shift from **reactive** to **proactive defense** and the importance of building **dynamic and flexible infrastructures** that can evolve in real-time to meet new challenges.

Understanding SDN, AI, and Access Control

At the core of a modern cyber defense infrastructure are three critical technologies: **Software Defined Networking (SDN), Artificial Intelligence (AI),** and **Access Control Systems**. These technologies form the building blocks for an adaptive and intelligent cybersecurity environment capable of responding to modern threats.

Software Defined Networking (SDN)

Software Defined Networking (SDN) is a revolutionary approach to managing and controlling network infrastructure. Unlike traditional networking, where hardware devices like routers and switches control both the **data plane** (which handles the actual transmission of packets) and the **control plane** (which dictates how packets are routed), SDN decouples these two functions. This separation enables **centralized control** over the entire network, allowing administrators to **programmatically manage** traffic flow based on real-time conditions and needs.

- **How SDN Works**:
  SDN uses a central **controller** to dictate how data flows through the network. This controller is programmable, meaning administrators can configure it to make dynamic decisions based on factors such as traffic patterns, security threats, or performance metrics. These decisions are then communicated to the network devices, which act accordingly by forwarding or rerouting traffic.
- **The Role of SDN in Cyber Defense**:
  SDN is critical in modern cyber defense for several reasons. First, it allows defenders to **dynamically segment** the network into isolated sections, making it harder for attackers to move laterally across the network after gaining initial access. This concept of **micro-segmentation** ensures that even if one part of the network is compromised, other sections remain insulated. Additionally, SDN can automatically reroute traffic in real-time to mitigate attacks, such as **DDoS** or **ransomware propagation**.
- **Benefits of SDN**:
  - **Flexibility**: SDN can quickly adapt to changing network conditions, such as scaling up to handle increased traffic or isolating compromised segments.
  - **Centralized Control**: Security policies can be enforced across the entire network from a single control point.
  - **Automation**: SDN allows for the automation of routine security tasks, such as traffic monitoring, filtering, and rerouting, enabling faster response to threats.

SDN is the foundation of a **dynamic defense strategy**, allowing organizations to quickly respond to and contain threats before they spread across the network.

ARTIFICIAL INTELLIGENCE (AI)

Artificial Intelligence (AI) has rapidly become a game-changer in the field of cybersecurity. Traditional security tools rely on predefined rules or **signatures** to detect known threats, but modern attackers often employ tactics that evade these static detection mechanisms. AI, particularly in the form of **machine learning (ML)** and **deep learning**, enables systems to detect anomalies and previously unseen threats by analyzing massive amounts of data in real-time.

- **How AI Works in Cyber Defense**:
  AI uses machine learning algorithms to study patterns in network traffic, user behavior, and system activities. Over time, these algorithms learn what constitutes "normal" activity within a given environment. When deviations from this norm occur—such as abnormal login times, unusual data transfers, or sudden spikes in traffic—AI can flag these anomalies as potential security incidents.
- **AI for Threat Detection**:
  One of the primary uses of AI in cybersecurity is in **real-time threat detection**. AI systems can analyze millions of data points from across the network, identifying patterns that would be impossible for human analysts to detect. By continuously learning from new data, AI systems can also detect **zero-day attacks**—new or unknown vulnerabilities that have not yet been addressed by traditional security tools.
- **AI-Driven Incident Response**:
  Beyond detecting threats, AI can also be integrated into **Security Orchestration, Automation, and Response (SOAR)** systems to automate the incident response process. When AI detects a potential threat, it can trigger automated actions, such as isolating affected systems, blocking malicious IP addresses, or initiating forensic analysis. This rapid, automated response minimizes the time between detection

and remediation, reducing the damage that attackers can cause.
- **Benefits of AI in Cyber Defense**:
    - **Speed and Scale**: AI can analyze vast amounts of data at speeds far beyond human capabilities.
    - **Proactive Defense**: AI can identify emerging threats and predict potential attack vectors before they are fully realized.
    - **Continuous Learning**: Machine learning algorithms improve over time, adapting to new attack techniques and evolving cyber threats.

AI's ability to **predict** and **respond** to threats in real-time makes it an essential component of any **proactive cyber defense strategy**.

ACCESS CONTROL SYSTEMS

Access control is one of the most fundamental elements of cybersecurity, governing **who** or **what** can access certain resources within a network. Traditional access control systems were often static, relying on predetermined rules and permissions. However, modern networks require more dynamic and **adaptive access control mechanisms** that can continuously verify users' identities and adjust access privileges in real-time.

- **How Access Control Works**:
  Access control systems determine whether users, devices, or applications are allowed to access specific resources within the network. This is typically managed through authentication (verifying the identity of the user) and authorization (determining whether the user has permission to access a particular resource).
- **Zero Trust and Dynamic Access Control**:
  In traditional models, once a user or device gained access to the network, they were often trusted implicitly, which led to **insider threats** or lateral movement after a breach. Modern cyber defense strategies adopt a **Zero Trust Architecture**

(ZTA), which operates on the principle of "never trust, always verify." This means that every access request—whether from inside or outside the network—must be continuously verified.

Access control is now **dynamic** and **contextual**, meaning it takes into account various factors such as the user's location, device, behavior, and time of access. **AI-driven continuous authentication** can monitor these factors in real-time, flagging suspicious behavior and adjusting access privileges accordingly.

- **Role in Micro-Segmentation**:
Access control plays a key role in **micro-segmentation**, a practice enabled by SDN. By dynamically managing access privileges and ensuring that users and devices can only access the resources they need, micro-segmentation limits the scope of potential damage from a breach.
- **Benefits of Modern Access Control Systems**:
    - **Continuous Verification**: Access is continuously verified at every step, reducing the likelihood of insider threats or lateral movement within the network.
    - **Contextual Decision-Making**: Access control decisions are based on real-time data, such as user behavior, location, and device health, allowing for more granular and intelligent security measures.
    - **Dynamic Response**: When suspicious behavior is detected, access controls can immediately revoke privileges, isolate users, or trigger multi-factor authentication (MFA).

Access control systems ensure that **only trusted users** and **devices** can interact with critical resources, acting as a gatekeeper that continuously adapts to evolving conditions.

Proactive vs. Reactive Defense

For many years, the dominant cybersecurity strategy was **reactive defense**—responding to threats only after they had been detected. This approach worked in a time when cyber threats were less sophisticated, and attackers relied on well-known tactics. However, in the modern threat landscape, **waiting for an attack to happen is no longer a viable strategy**. Instead, organizations must adopt a **proactive defense posture** that anticipates, detects, and mitigates threats before they fully manifest.

REACTIVE DEFENSE

In a **reactive defense** model, security teams focus on **identifying** and **responding to attacks** after they have already occurred. This often involves analyzing log data, investigating alerts from intrusion detection systems, and responding to breaches once they are detected.

- **Challenges of Reactive Defense:**
    - **Late Detection:** By the time a breach is identified, the attacker may have already exfiltrated data or caused significant damage.
    - **Manual Response:** Reactive defense often requires human intervention, leading to delays in responding to incidents and increasing the potential damage.
    - **Limited to Known Threats:** Reactive defense relies heavily on signature-based detection and predefined rules, making it ineffective against **zero-day attacks** or novel threats that do not match existing signatures.

PROACTIVE DEFENSE

In contrast, **proactive defense** is about **staying ahead of attackers** by continuously monitoring the environment for threats, hunting for vulnerabilities before they can be exploited, and leveraging AI and automation to detect and respond to threats in real time.

- **Threat Hunting**: Proactive defense involves actively **searching for threats** within the network, even if no indicators of compromise (IoCs) have been detected. This can include analyzing user behavior, monitoring for anomalous traffic patterns, and identifying vulnerabilities that could be exploited in the future.
- **Predictive Analytics**: AI and machine learning can be used to **predict future attacks** by analyzing historical data and identifying patterns that suggest an impending attack. For example, if an attacker is probing a network for weaknesses, AI systems can identify these patterns and alert security teams before the attacker moves to the next stage of their attack.
- **Real-Time Response**: In a proactive defense strategy, **incident response** is automated, enabling real-time mitigation of threats. For example, if an AI system detects an anomaly that indicates a potential breach, it can immediately take action to isolate the affected system, block malicious IP addresses, or trigger an investigation.
- **Continuous Adaptation**: Proactive defense also involves continuously **adapting security measures** based on the evolving threat landscape. This means regularly updating policies, patching vulnerabilities, and evolving security configurations to stay ahead of attackers.

THE IMPORTANCE OF DYNAMIC AND FLEXIBLE INFRASTRUCTURES

To support a proactive defense strategy, organizations must build **dynamic** and **flexible infrastructures** that can rapidly adapt to changing conditions. Static, rigid infrastructures are easy targets for attackers because they do not evolve with the threat landscape. In contrast, dynamic infrastructures, powered by technologies like SDN and AI, can change in real-time to mitigate attacks, isolate threats, and ensure business continuity.

FLEXIBILITY IN NETWORK INFRASTRUCTURE

Traditional network infrastructures are often hardwired, with predefined routes, static security configurations, and limited ability to adapt. **Dynamic infrastructures** leverage **SDN** to make real-time adjustments to traffic flow, network segmentation, and access controls.

- **Real-Time Reconfiguration**: In the event of an attack, SDN can dynamically **reconfigure the network** to reroute traffic away from compromised systems, isolate suspicious segments, or deploy additional security controls to high-risk areas.
- **Automated Failover**: In dynamic infrastructures, **failover mechanisms** are automated. If one part of the network is compromised or experiences a failure, traffic can be automatically redirected to backup systems or alternate routes, ensuring minimal disruption to operations.

SCALABILITY AND RESILIENCE

Dynamic infrastructures are also inherently **scalable**, allowing organizations to **add or remove resources** as needed. This is particularly important in **cloud environments**, where workloads can be dynamically scaled based on demand.

- **Resilience through Redundancy**: Dynamic infrastructures are designed with **redundancy** in mind. By creating multiple pathways for traffic and deploying backups for critical systems, dynamic infrastructures can recover quickly from attacks or system failures.
- **Elastic Security**: Just as dynamic infrastructures can scale in response to demand, they can also scale **security measures**. For example, if an AI system detects a DDoS attack, the infrastructure can automatically allocate additional resources to handle the increased traffic, while security systems deploy extra firewalls or filters to block malicious requests.

AGILITY IN RESPONSE TO THREATS

A key feature of dynamic infrastructures is their **agility** in responding to new threats. In static environments, attackers can easily map out the network and identify weak points. In dynamic environments, the network's topology and security measures are constantly shifting, making it much harder for attackers to gain a foothold.

- **Micro-Segmentation**: One of the most effective ways to prevent lateral movement within a network is through **micro-segmentation**. By using SDN to create isolated zones within the network, dynamic infrastructures can ensure that even if an attacker breaches one part of the system, they cannot easily move to other areas.
- **Adaptive Access Control**: Access control in dynamic infrastructures is also adaptive. AI-driven systems can adjust access privileges based on **contextual factors** like location, device health, and behavior, ensuring that users only have access to what they need at any given time.

CONCLUSION: BUILDING THE FOUNDATION FOR MODERN CYBER DEFENSE

In today's rapidly evolving threat landscape, static defenses and reactive strategies are no longer enough to protect organizations from sophisticated cyberattacks. To defend against modern threats, organizations must adopt a proactive, flexible, and dynamic approach to cybersecurity. Technologies like **Software Defined Networking (SDN), Artificial Intelligence (AI),** and **Access Control Systems** form the backbone of this modern defense strategy, enabling organizations to detect, respond to, and mitigate threats in real-time.

By embracing **proactive defense strategies**, leveraging **AI for real-time threat detection**, and building **dynamic infrastructures** that can adapt to changing conditions, organizations can stay ahead of attackers and ensure the security and resilience of their networks. This chapter provides the foundation for the more advanced strategies that will be explored in the following sections, emphasizing the need for agility, adaptability, and innovation in modern cyber defense.

CHAPTER 2: GUERRILLA WARFARE IN CYBERSPACE

INTRODUCTION

In the world of cyber defense, organizations are increasingly facing adversaries with superior resources, advanced tools, and the advantage of surprise. In this asymmetrical environment, defenders need to abandon the idea of static, resource-intensive defenses and adopt the tactics of **guerrilla warfare**—a strategy historically employed by smaller forces against a more powerful opponent. Guerrilla warfare is characterized by **mobility, agility, deception**, and **unpredictability**, with an emphasis on avoiding direct confrontation and instead exploiting the enemy's weaknesses.

The principles of guerrilla warfare, when applied to **cybersecurity**, offer a compelling framework for defenders to **level the playing field** against nation-state attackers, organized cybercriminal syndicates, and highly sophisticated hacking collectives. In cyberspace, where adversaries can strike from anywhere, defenders must adopt **guerrilla-style tactics** to remain agile, unpredictable, and proactive in disrupting attacks.

This chapter will provide an overview of the key principles of guerrilla warfare and show how these can be applied to **cyber**

defense to create more flexible, adaptive, and resilient strategies. The importance of **deception, flexibility,** and **surprise** will be emphasized as essential elements for defenders to keep attackers off balance and neutralize threats effectively.

Overview of Guerrilla Warfare Principles

Guerrilla warfare is not about overwhelming the enemy with sheer force. Instead, it focuses on using **asymmetry** to strike at the enemy's weakest points, avoiding direct confrontations where the attacker holds the advantage. These tactics have been used throughout history by smaller, less-equipped forces to outmaneuver and wear down larger adversaries. The key principles of guerrilla warfare can be broken down into the following:

1. AGILITY AND MOBILITY

In traditional warfare, guerrilla fighters rely on **speed** and **mobility** to stay ahead of their enemies. They move quickly, strike unexpectedly, and retreat before the enemy can respond. This tactic is crucial for avoiding prolonged engagements with a superior force that could overwhelm them.

In the context of cyber defense, **agility** refers to the ability to respond quickly to threats, change security measures on the fly, and **adapt defenses in real time**. Cyber defenders must be able to detect, isolate, and neutralize threats before they can escalate into full-scale breaches. This requires dynamic systems that can be reconfigured instantly based on real-time intelligence.

- **Key principle**: Strike quickly, adapt faster, and retreat from static defensive positions. Defenders must use technologies like **SDN** and **AI** to create agile, rapidly reconfigurable networks and defenses that keep attackers guessing and unable to pin down weaknesses.

2. DECEPTION AND MISDIRECTION

Guerrilla forces often use **deception** to confuse, mislead, and frustrate their enemies. They may deploy decoys, misinformation, and false targets to lure their opponents into traps or distract them from real objectives. The goal is to make the enemy waste time and resources on false leads, ultimately creating openings for the guerrillas to exploit.

In cybersecurity, **deception tactics** such as **honeypots, honeynets,** and **decoy systems** serve a similar purpose. By deploying decoy environments that mimic real systems, defenders can lure attackers into engaging with fake assets, thus diverting them away from critical infrastructure and gaining valuable intelligence about their tools and methods.

- **Key principle**: Confuse and mislead the attacker with **false targets** and **decoys**. Make the enemy chase after phantom systems while the real assets remain secure, collecting intelligence from their interactions with the fake environment.

3. ASYMMETRY AND TARGETING VULNERABILITIES

Guerrilla warfare is inherently asymmetric, meaning it seeks to exploit the vulnerabilities of a more powerful opponent. Rather than engaging in head-to-head battles, guerrilla fighters strike at the enemy's weak points—often targeting supply lines, communications, or isolated outposts—where the adversary is less prepared or defended.

In cyber defense, this means **targeting the attacker's infrastructure** and **weak points**, such as **command-and-control (C2) servers**, **malware distribution channels**, or **exploitable systems** within the attacker's environment. This tactic can involve disrupting the tools the attackers use, attacking their communications, or even launching **preemptive strikes** to neutralize an adversary's capabilities before they can act.

- **Key principle**: Avoid direct confrontation. Instead, exploit the adversary's weaknesses and disrupt their infrastructure to prevent them from gaining a foothold or achieving their objectives.

4. THE ELEMENT OF SURPRISE

Surprise is one of the most effective weapons in guerrilla warfare. By attacking at unexpected times and in unexpected places, guerrilla forces keep their enemies off balance, forcing them to spread their resources thin and respond to attacks in multiple locations. This unpredictability frustrates the adversary and forces them into a defensive posture.

In the digital domain, the **element of surprise** is equally powerful. Attackers rely on predictability and routine in the defenses they encounter, mapping out systems and looking for static vulnerabilities to exploit. By constantly **changing configurations**, **rotating security keys**, and employing **randomized defenses**, cyber defenders can ensure that attackers are never sure of what they are facing.

- **Key principle**: Keep the enemy off balance by being **unpredictable**. Use dynamic security configurations and randomization to prevent attackers from successfully mapping or exploiting your defenses.

5. HIT-AND-RUN TACTICS

In guerrilla warfare, forces strike quickly, inflict damage, and retreat before the enemy can respond. The goal is to minimize the risk of direct confrontation and limit exposure to counterattacks, while still causing significant disruption to the enemy's operations.

Cyber defenders can apply **hit-and-run tactics** by rapidly **isolating compromised systems**, **cutting off attackers' access**, and **neutralizing threats** before they can fully establish control. The use of **automated incident response systems** can help security teams to act quickly by quarantine infected systems, block malicious traffic, and thwart ongoing attacks before they escalate.

- **Key principle**: Strike hard and fast, then retreat to re-evaluate and reposition. Ensure that security systems are capable of immediate response and that threats are neutralized before they spread.

Applying Guerrilla Tactics to Cyber Defense

The principles of guerrilla warfare can be directly translated into the realm of cybersecurity, offering defenders a tactical advantage even when facing more sophisticated or better-resourced adversaries. Let's explore how each of these guerrilla warfare principles can be applied to **cyber defense** in practical ways.

1. AGILITY AND MOBILITY IN CYBER DEFENSE

In cyberspace, attackers often rely on **static defenses** to gather information and plan their attacks. The longer defenders remain in a fixed, unchanging posture, the easier it is for attackers to map the environment, identify weaknesses, and exploit vulnerabilities. To counter this, cyber defenders must prioritize **agility** and **mobility**, just as guerrilla fighters do in traditional warfare.

- **SDN for Dynamic Network Segmentation**:
  Using **Software Defined Networking (SDN)**, defenders can **dynamically segment their networks** in real-time, creating isolated zones that prevent attackers from moving laterally once they gain initial access. SDN allows defenders to quickly reconfigure network topology, isolate threats, and reroute traffic, making it difficult for attackers to predict or exploit vulnerabilities.
- **AI-Driven Automation for Instant Response**:
  Artificial Intelligence (AI) can help automate responses to threats, allowing defenders to **quickly adjust access controls**, apply patches, or block malicious activity without manual intervention. This kind of speed and agility is critical when

facing fast-moving threats like **ransomware** or **DDoS attacks**, where every second counts.
- **Micro-Segmentation and Rapid Containment:**
By deploying **micro-segmentation**, defenders can limit the spread of an attack by isolating compromised systems from the rest of the network. This limits the scope of an attacker's control and allows for faster containment and recovery.

2. DECEPTION AND MISDIRECTION: CONFUSING THE ADVERSARY

Just as guerrilla fighters use decoys and misinformation to mislead their enemies, cyber defenders can use **deception technologies** to **confuse attackers**, waste their resources, and gain valuable intelligence.

- **Honeypots and Honeynets:**
Honeypots are decoy systems designed to attract attackers by simulating vulnerable systems. When an attacker engages with a honeypot, they believe they are interacting with a legitimate system, but in reality, they are being monitored by defenders. This allows defenders to gather **intelligence on the attacker's tactics**, tools, and objectives, all while keeping the real systems safe. **Honeynets** extend this idea by creating entire fake networks filled with decoys to further mislead attackers.
- **Deceptive File Systems and Fake Credentials:**
Cyber defenders can also deploy **deceptive file systems**, where fake data and credentials are placed in strategic locations to entice attackers. These decoy assets can be configured to alert security teams when accessed, providing early warning of an intruder's presence and intentions.
- **Dynamic Misdirection:**
Through **SDN** and other dynamic technologies, defenders can set up **ambush zones** within their network—areas designed to attract attackers and trap them in fake environments. As the attacker navigates these zones, defenders can gather

critical intelligence or deploy countermeasures to neutralize the threat.

3. EXPLOITING ASYMMETRY IN CYBER DEFENSE

In guerrilla warfare, the goal is to exploit the vulnerabilities of a stronger adversary by avoiding direct confrontation and attacking their weakest points. In the cyber world, defenders can employ **asymmetric tactics** to disrupt an attacker's operations and neutralize their ability to execute successful attacks.

- **Targeting Attack Infrastructure**:
  Many cyberattacks rely on **command-and-control (C2) infrastructure**, which attackers use to coordinate their efforts, deploy malware, and exfiltrate data. By **disrupting these infrastructure components**, defenders can cripple the attacker's ability to maintain control over compromised systems. This might involve using intelligence to identify and take down C2 servers or working with law enforcement to dismantle **botnets** used by attackers.
- **Exploiting Attacker Overconfidence**:
  Attackers often rely on the assumption that defenders will follow predictable patterns or that certain systems are vulnerable. By leveraging **AI to predict attack patterns** or deploying **cyber deception**, defenders can exploit these assumptions to trick attackers into revealing their intentions or making costly mistakes.

4. THE ELEMENT OF SURPRISE IN CYBER DEFENSE

Just as guerrilla fighters rely on surprise to keep their enemies off balance, cyber defenders can use **unpredictability** as a key tactic to thwart attackers.

- **Rotating Security Keys and Access Controls**:
  One way to introduce **unpredictability** into cyber defense is by regularly **rotating encryption keys**, **access controls**, and

other security credentials. Attackers who attempt to exploit stolen credentials will find that these are no longer valid, frustrating their efforts and forcing them to start over.

- **Randomized Security Configurations**:
By continuously **shuffling network configurations**, defenders can prevent attackers from successfully mapping the environment or identifying static vulnerabilities. SDN enables this kind of flexibility, allowing defenders to regularly change the architecture of the network without disrupting normal operations.

- **AI-Driven Anomaly Detection**:
AI systems can be programmed to **randomly alter security parameters**, such as adjusting firewall rules or reconfiguring access permissions, based on real-time analysis of network traffic. This creates an environment where attackers can never be sure of what defenses they will face, forcing them to expend significant effort just to understand the current security posture.

5. HIT-AND-RUN TACTICS IN CYBER DEFENSE

The concept of **hit-and-run tactics** can be applied to cyber defense in the form of **rapid response** and **isolation of compromised systems**. Rather than allowing attackers to gain a foothold and move laterally through the network, defenders can **strike quickly** to neutralize the threat before it escalates.

- **Automated Incident Response**:
Modern **Security Orchestration, Automation, and Response (SOAR)** systems can automate many aspects of incident response, ensuring that threats are detected, isolated, and mitigated within seconds of being identified. This prevents attackers from maintaining control over compromised systems and limits the damage they can cause.

- **Quarantine and Reconfigure**:
Once a threat is detected, defenders can use **SDN** to quickly **quarantine compromised systems**, rerouting traffic away

from affected areas and **reconfiguring the network** to prevent further attacks. This approach ensures that the defender can **contain the attack** before it spreads, much like guerrilla forces striking at a target and then retreating to safety.

Flexibility, Deception, and the Element of Surprise

At the heart of guerrilla warfare—both in traditional and cyber contexts—are the principles of **flexibility**, **deception**, and **the element of surprise**. These tactics allow defenders to remain agile, unpredictable, and in control, even when facing a stronger adversary.

FLEXIBILITY

In cyber defense, flexibility is the ability to **adapt defenses in real time** based on the evolving nature of an attack. With tools like **SDN**, defenders can continuously **adjust the network environment** to make it harder for attackers to find a foothold. By ensuring that security measures are **dynamic** rather than static, defenders can maintain the upper hand.

DECEPTION

Deception is a powerful tool for keeping attackers off balance. By deploying **decoys, false data,** and **misleading signals**, defenders can lure attackers into making mistakes, reveal their tactics, or waste valuable time chasing after false targets. Deception allows defenders to **shape the battlefield** on their terms.

THE ELEMENT OF SURPRISE

The element of surprise ensures that attackers are **constantly guessing**. Whether through **randomized security configurations**, rotating access credentials, or AI-driven anomaly detection, defenders must remain **unpredictable** to disrupt the attacker's strategy and force them into a defensive posture.

CONCLUSION: GUERRILLA TACTICS AS A FORCE MULTIPLIER IN CYBER DEFENSE

In today's cyber threat landscape, defenders must **think like guerrilla fighters**, employing agility, deception, and surprise to **outmaneuver more powerful adversaries**. By embracing **dynamic defense strategies**, leveraging tools like **SDN** and **AI**, and applying the **principles of guerrilla warfare** to cybersecurity, defenders can turn the tables on attackers, keeping them off balance and unable to achieve their objectives.

CHAPTER 3: HIT-AND-RUN TACTICS IN CYBERWARFARE

INTRODUCTION

In traditional guerrilla warfare, the **hit-and-run tactic** has been one of the most effective methods used by smaller, less-equipped forces to disrupt and wear down more powerful adversaries. It involves **striking quickly**, inflicting damage, and retreating before the enemy can mount a counterattack. This tactic thrives on **surprise, speed, and mobility**, enabling guerrilla fighters to capitalize on the enemy's vulnerabilities while avoiding prolonged engagements that could lead to their defeat.

In the realm of **cyberwarfare**, the principles of hit-and-run are equally applicable. Cyber defenders often face adversaries with superior resources, time, and technological advantage, such as nation-state attackers, organized cybercrime groups, or sophisticated hacking collectives. However, by adopting **cyber hit-and-run tactics**, defenders can neutralize threats quickly and prevent attackers from gaining a foothold within their networks. The ability to swiftly **isolate, contain,** and **neutralize** threats before they escalate is crucial to modern cyber defense.

In this chapter, we will explore how **hit-and-run tactics** from traditional guerrilla warfare translate into **cyberspace**, focusing on **quick isolation and containment of threats using Software Defined Networking (SDN)**. We will also examine **real-world examples** of these tactics in action, demonstrating their effectiveness in preventing large-scale breaches and minimizing damage.

The Concept of Hit-and-Run in Traditional Guerrilla Warfare

The **hit-and-run** tactic is one of the most recognized strategies in traditional guerrilla warfare, employed by smaller, less-equipped forces to achieve tactical victories against larger, more powerful opponents. The key elements of this tactic are **speed, surprise, and mobility**. Guerrilla fighters strike at vulnerable points, such as enemy supply lines, isolated patrols, or weak outposts, inflict damage, and then quickly withdraw before the enemy can retaliate. The goal is not to win a decisive battle but to create cumulative disruptions that weaken the enemy over time.

KEY PRINCIPLES OF HIT-AND-RUN IN GUERRILLA WARFARE

1. **Speed and Mobility**:
   In hit-and-run tactics, guerrilla fighters must move swiftly. They attack a target, causing maximum disruption in the shortest amount of time, and retreat before the enemy can organize a counterattack. This speed and mobility allow the guerrilla forces to avoid drawn-out battles, where their

smaller numbers and limited resources would put them at a disadvantage.

2. **Targeting Weaknesses**:
Guerrilla fighters identify **vulnerable points** in the enemy's defenses. These could be supply convoys, communication infrastructure, or isolated units. By attacking the weak points, they can cause significant damage with minimal risk.

3. **Avoiding Direct Confrontation**:
Guerrilla forces rarely engage in direct, head-to-head confrontations with larger forces. Instead, they rely on the element of surprise to strike quickly and withdraw before the enemy can retaliate, minimizing their exposure to counterattacks.

4. **Cumulative Disruption**:
Hit-and-run tactics are not designed to win a war through a single engagement. Instead, they create a **war of attrition**, where the enemy is gradually weakened through a series of small, disruptive attacks. Over time, these small attacks can erode the enemy's morale, resources, and ability to wage war effectively.

In traditional guerrilla warfare, hit-and-run tactics allow smaller forces to remain elusive, unpredictable, and effective against larger adversaries, creating a dynamic and fluid battlefield where the enemy struggles to respond.

How Hit-and-Run Tactics Translate into Cyberspace

In the context of **cyberwarfare**, hit-and-run tactics can be adapted to help defenders respond to cyber threats in a **fast, dynamic, and fluid** manner. Just as guerrilla fighters strike quickly and retreat, cyber defenders can use hit-and-run tactics to **detect**, **isolate**, and **contain threats** before they have the opportunity to cause significant damage.

Cyber hit-and-run tactics are focused on **rapid response** to cyber threats. These tactics leverage **real-time threat detection, automated incident response,** and **dynamic network reconfiguration** to neutralize threats and prevent attackers from gaining a foothold. By striking quickly—isolating compromised systems or blocking malicious activity—and then retreating to reassess and reconfigure defenses, cyber defenders can prevent threats from escalating into full-scale breaches.

1. RAPID THREAT DETECTION AND RESPONSE

The first step in cyber hit-and-run tactics is the ability to **rapidly detect** and **respond** to threats. This requires **real-time monitoring** and **automated detection** mechanisms capable of identifying malicious activity as soon as it occurs. Tools like **Artificial Intelligence (AI)** and **machine learning** play a crucial role in this process, enabling defenders to detect **anomalies** and **suspicious behavior** that may indicate the presence of a threat.

- **AI-Powered Anomaly Detection**:
  AI systems can analyze network traffic and user behavior in real time, flagging deviations from normal patterns that may signal a cyberattack. For example, if a user suddenly begins downloading large amounts of sensitive data outside of normal working hours, AI-driven systems can automatically detect this anomaly and initiate a response.
- **Automated Incident Response**:
  Once a threat is detected, **automated incident response systems** can take immediate action. These systems are designed to **isolate compromised systems**, block malicious traffic, or trigger alerts to security teams for further investigation. By automating the response process, cyber defenders can neutralize threats before they escalate.

2. ISOLATION AND CONTAINMENT

In hit-and-run tactics, **isolation and containment** are the primary objectives. The goal is to prevent the threat from spreading across the network by quickly isolating the affected systems and containing the damage. This approach ensures that the rest of the network remains secure while the compromised system is quarantined for further investigation.

- **Quarantining Infected Systems**:
  When a system is compromised, hit-and-run tactics involve **immediately isolating** that system from the rest of the network. This prevents attackers from using the compromised system to launch further attacks or move laterally within the network. **Software Defined Networking (SDN)** allows for **dynamic reconfiguration**, enabling defenders to quickly quarantine affected systems and limit the attack's scope.
- **Containment of Lateral Movement**:
  Attackers often attempt to move laterally within a network to access more critical systems. Hit-and-run tactics prevent this by employing **micro-segmentation**—a technique where the network is divided into isolated segments, and communication between those segments is tightly controlled. If an attacker gains access to one segment, they are prevented from accessing other segments, limiting the damage.

3. RETREAT, RECONFIGURE, AND REASSESS

After a system is isolated and the immediate threat is contained, defenders must **retreat, reconfigure**, and **reassess** their defenses. This step involves investigating the threat, gathering intelligence on the attacker's methods, and adjusting the network configuration to prevent similar attacks in the future.

- **Post-Incident Analysis**:
  Once the immediate threat is neutralized, defenders can conduct a **forensic investigation** to determine how the attack occurred, what vulnerabilities were exploited, and whether any data was exfiltrated. This intelligence is crucial for improving future defenses and closing any security gaps.
- **Reconfiguration of Network Segments**:
  SDN enables defenders to quickly reconfigure network segments in response to an attack. After isolating a compromised system, the network topology can be adjusted to further limit the attacker's ability to move within the network. This dynamic reconfiguration makes it harder for attackers to plan future attacks, as the network environment is constantly changing.
- **Adaptive Defense**:
  Hit-and-run tactics in cyberspace are not about maintaining a static defense posture. Instead, they emphasize **adaptive defense**, where the network's security measures evolve in response to the attack. Defenders must continuously adjust their defenses based on the intelligence gathered during each attack, ensuring that the network remains resilient against evolving threats.

QUICK ISOLATION AND CONTAINMENT OF THREATS USING SDN

Software Defined Networking (SDN) plays a critical role in the successful application of hit-and-run tactics in cyber defense. SDN allows defenders to **dynamically manage and reconfigure** their network infrastructure in real time, enabling rapid **isolation and containment** of threats. By leveraging SDN's ability to **centralize control** over the network, defenders can quickly respond to threats and ensure that attackers are unable to spread laterally within the network.

HOW SDN ENABLES HIT-AND-RUN TACTICS

1. **Real-Time Network Segmentation**:
   One of the key advantages of SDN is its ability to perform **real-time segmentation** of the network. When a threat is detected, SDN controllers can automatically create **micro-segments** around the compromised system, isolating it from the rest of the network. This prevents the attacker from moving to other systems and allows defenders to focus on neutralizing the threat without worrying about it spreading.
2. **Automated Traffic Rerouting**:
   In addition to isolating compromised systems, SDN enables defenders to **reroute network traffic** away from the affected area. This ensures that critical business operations can continue uninterrupted while the compromised system is dealt with. By dynamically adjusting the flow of traffic, SDN reduces the impact of the attack and ensures that attackers are unable to access other parts of the network.
3. **Flexible Security Policy Enforcement**:
   SDN allows for **centralized control** over the network's security policies. This means that defenders can quickly update or change security rules in response to an attack. For example, if a particular segment of the network is compromised, SDN can enforce stricter access controls or firewall rules in that area to limit the attacker's ability to communicate with other systems.
4. **Dynamic Defense Mechanisms**:
   SDN provides the flexibility to implement **dynamic defense mechanisms**, such as **adaptive firewalls, moving target defense**, and **automated intrusion prevention systems (IPS)**. These defenses can be quickly deployed or reconfigured to respond to emerging threats, ensuring that the attacker is constantly facing new obstacles.

SDN IN ACTION: A HIT-AND-RUN SCENARIO

Imagine a scenario where a cyberattack is detected in a corporate network. Using traditional network management techniques, isolating the compromised system would be slow and labor-intensive, giving the attacker time to move laterally and compromise additional systems. However, with SDN, defenders can instantly isolate the infected system by creating a **quarantine zone** around it.

- **Step 1: Detection**:
  An AI-driven monitoring system detects abnormal behavior on a workstation that indicates it has been compromised by malware.
- **Step 2: Isolation**:
  SDN controllers immediately isolate the infected workstation by creating a micro-segment around it. All traffic to and from the compromised system is blocked, and the workstation is quarantined.
- **Step 3: Rerouting**:
  Network traffic is rerouted to bypass the compromised area, ensuring that business operations continue without disruption.
- **Step 4: Reconfiguration**:
  Security policies are updated to enforce stricter access controls within the quarantined segment. Firewalls are adjusted to block any further attempts by the attacker to move laterally.
- **Step 5: Analysis and Response**:
  A forensic investigation is launched to analyze the malware and determine how the system was compromised. Once the threat is fully neutralized, the system is restored to normal operation.

This **rapid isolation and containment** using SDN ensures that the attack is neutralized quickly, limiting the damage and preventing the attacker from compromising additional systems.

EXAMPLES OF REAL-WORLD HIT-AND-RUN TACTICS IN CYBER DEFENSE

Several real-world cyber incidents have demonstrated the effectiveness of hit-and-run tactics in minimizing the impact of cyberattacks. These examples show how **quick isolation, containment, and dynamic response** can prevent widespread damage and help defenders regain control of their networks.

1. WANNACRY RANSOMWARE ATTACK (2017)

In 2017, the **WannaCry ransomware** attack spread rapidly across global networks, encrypting files on infected systems and demanding payment in Bitcoin for decryption. While many organizations were caught off guard, those with **dynamic network segmentation** and **automated incident response** were able to quickly contain the spread of the ransomware.

- **Hit-and-Run Tactics in Action**:
  Some organizations used **SDN** to rapidly **quarantine infected systems**, preventing the ransomware from propagating across the network. By isolating compromised systems and blocking malicious traffic, they were able to minimize the damage and restore normal operations more quickly than those without dynamic defenses.

2. SOLARWINDS SUPPLY CHAIN ATTACK (2020)

The **SolarWinds attack** was a sophisticated supply chain attack that compromised numerous government agencies and private organizations by infiltrating SolarWinds' software updates. The attackers remained undetected for months, moving laterally within networks and exfiltrating sensitive data.

- **Hit-and-Run Tactics in Action**:
  Organizations that employed **micro-segmentation** and **dynamic reconfiguration** were able to limit the attackers' lateral movement. By quickly identifying compromised systems and isolating them,

they prevented the attackers from gaining access to more critical parts of the network.

3. Maersk NotPetya Attack (2017)

In 2017, the global shipping company Maersk was hit by the NotPetya malware, which severely disrupted its operations worldwide. Although the attack crippled critical systems, Maersk managed to recover relatively quickly by rapidly rebuilding its infrastructure and utilizing backups.

- **Hit-and-Run Tactics in Action**:
  After detecting the attack, Maersk's IT teams moved swiftly to isolate compromised systems and manually restore critical network functions. The company leveraged its backup systems, including a fortunate discovery of an offline domain controller in Ghana, which allowed for a more rapid rebuild of its global IT infrastructure. By quickly segmenting and containing affected parts of the network, Maersk was able to resume most of its operations within 10 days, minimizing the overall damage. The agility and rapid response of Maersk's recovery efforts are akin to "guerrilla tactics," focusing on isolating damage, restoring key functions, and recovering quickly after the initial disruption.

Conclusion: Hit-and-Run Tactics as a Cyber Defense Strategy

The principles of **hit-and-run tactics** from traditional guerrilla warfare are highly effective when applied to **cyber defense**. By focusing on **rapid detection, quick isolation**, and **dynamic containment**, defenders can neutralize threats before they escalate, minimizing the impact of cyberattacks and preventing attackers from gaining a foothold within their networks.

In cyberspace, tools like **SDN** and **AI** enable defenders to execute hit-and-run tactics with precision and speed, ensuring that their networks remain agile, flexible, and resilient. As demonstrated by real-world examples, these tactics are essential for organizations looking to stay ahead of sophisticated cyber adversaries and maintain control of their environments.

CHAPTER 4: ASYMMETRY: LEVERAGING SMALL, AGILE TEAMS AGAINST LARGE THREAT ACTORS

Introduction

In traditional warfare, smaller forces often face overwhelming odds when pitted against more powerful adversaries such as larger armies or well-funded nations. This is equally true in the realm of **cyber conflict**, where **nation-state attackers** and **organized crime syndicates** often possess vastly superior resources, including cutting-edge tools, large teams of skilled operators, and seemingly limitless time to plan and execute their attacks.

For defenders—especially those in small and medium-sized organizations, or even small cybersecurity teams within larger enterprises—the challenge can seem insurmountable. However, **asymmetric strategies** can level the playing field. Asymmetric warfare, by its nature, involves using unconventional methods to exploit the vulnerabilities of a more powerful adversary. In cyber conflict, small, agile teams can use these tactics to **outmaneuver** and **disrupt** larger threat actors, turning the attacker's strengths into weaknesses.

This chapter will explore the concept of **asymmetry in cyber conflict**, demonstrating how small teams can effectively defend against powerful adversaries such as **nation-states** or **organized cybercrime**. We will also examine how asymmetric strategies allow defenders to identify and exploit the weaknesses of their attackers, and review **case studies** of successful asymmetric cyber defenses against **Advanced Persistent Threats (APTs)**.

Understanding Asymmetry in Cyber Conflict

Asymmetry in warfare refers to situations where two opposing forces are vastly unequal in terms of size, strength, resources, or technology. In such cases, the smaller, weaker force often cannot engage in direct confrontation with the larger opponent without suffering significant losses. Instead, the smaller force employs **unconventional tactics** designed to exploit the larger opponent's weaknesses. This could include targeting supply lines, conducting guerrilla raids, or using surprise attacks to keep the larger force off balance.

In **cyber conflict**, asymmetry takes on a different form. The larger adversaries—such as nation-states and organized crime syndicates—often have substantial resources at their disposal, including:

- **Advanced cyber tools**: Nation-states may possess **zero-day exploits**, custom-built malware, and sophisticated intrusion tools that are far beyond the capabilities of most small security teams.
- **Skilled personnel**: These larger adversaries often have teams of highly trained professionals, including **hackers**, **data scientists**, and **malware developers**, working together to achieve their objectives.
- **Time and persistence**: Advanced Persistent Threats (APTs), particularly those backed by nation-states, often have the luxury of time. They can spend months, or even years, infiltrating and maintaining persistence within a network, gathering intelligence and moving laterally through systems without detection.

Despite these overwhelming advantages, small teams are not defenseless. By adopting **asymmetric tactics**, defenders can negate some of these advantages and force attackers into making mistakes. Asymmetry in cyber defense involves:

1. **Agility**: Small teams can move quickly, adapt defenses in real-time, and respond to emerging threats without the bureaucratic delays that often hamper larger organizations.
2. **Targeted Defenses**: Small teams can focus their limited resources on protecting their most critical assets, rather than spreading defenses thin across an entire network.
3. **Exploiting Attacker Weaknesses**: Attackers, no matter how sophisticated, have weaknesses that defenders can exploit. These may include reliance on predictable tactics, overconfidence, or the use of specific infrastructure (such as **command-and-control servers**) that can be disrupted.

By understanding these asymmetries, defenders can turn the tide in their favor, even when facing a much more powerful adversary.

How Small Teams Can Defend Against Nation-States or Organized Crime

While large organizations and nation-state attackers have the benefit of extensive resources, smaller cybersecurity teams have several key advantages that can make them highly effective at **defending against large-scale attacks**. The success of small teams hinges on their ability to use **speed**, **specialization**, and **flexibility** to outmaneuver their adversaries.

1. SPEED AND AGILITY

One of the greatest advantages that smaller teams have over large adversaries is **speed**. Small teams can often make decisions and implement changes far more quickly than their larger counterparts. In many cases, the attackers themselves—especially those operating under the constraints of bureaucratic nation-states—must follow strict procedures, get approvals for certain actions, or rely on complex infrastructure to coordinate their attacks.

- **Rapid Decision Making**: Small teams can **react to threats** in real time, immediately deploying countermeasures without needing to go through layers of approval. This speed is particularly useful when dealing with **zero-day attacks** or ongoing breaches, where time is of the essence.
- **Real-Time Adaptation**: Because small teams are not bound by rigid processes, they can adapt defenses **on the fly**, using **AI** and **automation** to reconfigure systems, apply patches, or change access controls based on real-time data.

2. TARGETED PROTECTION OF CRITICAL ASSETS

Large organizations often struggle to protect every system and asset within their network, leading to vulnerabilities in areas that may not receive enough attention. Small teams, on the other hand, can focus their efforts on **high-value assets**, ensuring that critical systems are fortified with the most robust security measures.

- **Prioritizing Defenses**: Instead of trying to defend an entire network, small teams can concentrate their defenses on **mission-critical systems** or **high-value data**, such as customer databases, intellectual property, or proprietary technologies.
- **Hardening Key Systems**: By **micro-segmenting** the network, deploying **multi-factor authentication (MFA)**, and using **encryption**, small teams can make it extremely difficult for attackers to access or exfiltrate critical data, even if other parts of the network are compromised.

3. DECEPTION AND MISDIRECTION

Small teams can employ **cyber deception tactics** to mislead attackers and divert their attention away from critical assets. By deploying **honeypots**, **decoy systems**, and **false credentials**, defenders can confuse attackers, gather intelligence on their methods, and disrupt their plans.

- **Honeypots and Decoy Systems**: These systems are designed to mimic real assets, tricking attackers into believing they have successfully breached the network. Meanwhile, defenders can observe the attack in progress, analyze the tools and techniques being used, and respond accordingly.
- **Misinformation Campaigns**: Small teams can use **misinformation** to make attackers believe they have accessed valuable data or credentials, only to realize too late that the information is false or tampered with. This tactic can waste the attacker's time and resources while giving the defenders a strategic advantage.

4. AUTOMATION AND AI

Small teams can compensate for their lack of manpower by leveraging **AI-driven automation** to perform tasks that would otherwise require human intervention. Automation can handle routine tasks such as **monitoring network traffic, detecting anomalies**, and **automating incident response**, freeing up human operators to focus on more strategic decision-making.

- **Automated Detection**: AI systems can detect **anomalous behavior** in real time, identifying suspicious activity that may indicate the presence of an attacker. This allows small teams to respond to threats much faster than they could manually.
- **Automated Response**: Once a threat is detected, **automated response systems** can take immediate action to isolate the compromised system, block malicious IP addresses, or revoke access privileges, significantly reducing the time between detection and mitigation.

Using Asymmetry to Identify and Exploit Adversary Weaknesses

No matter how powerful an adversary is, there are always **weaknesses** that can be exploited. Large, well-resourced threat actors—whether they are nation-states or organized crime groups—are not invincible. Their size, complexity, and reliance on specific infrastructure often create opportunities for smaller teams to strike back.

1. OVERCONFIDENCE AND PREDICTABILITY

Sophisticated attackers may sometimes fall into the trap of **overconfidence**, believing that their size and capabilities make them untouchable. This overconfidence can lead them to make mistakes or become predictable in their tactics. **Nation-state attackers**, for example, may rely on the same infrastructure (such as **command-and-control (C2) servers**) for multiple operations, making them vulnerable to disruption.

- **Exploiting Reused Infrastructure**: Many nation-state attackers reuse the same C2 infrastructure across different campaigns. Small teams can use **threat intelligence** to identify these infrastructure components and work with law enforcement or industry partners to **disrupt** or **takedown** C2 servers, effectively cutting off the attacker's ability to coordinate further actions.
- **Pattern Recognition**: Using AI-driven systems to **analyze attacker behavior**, small teams can identify **predictable attack patterns**. By learning how attackers approach specific targets, defenders can preemptively adjust their defenses to neutralize the threat before it materializes.

2. TARGETING COMMAND-AND-CONTROL (C2) SERVERS

Many advanced cyberattacks rely on **C2 servers** to maintain communication between compromised systems and the attacker. These servers play a critical role in coordinating malware operations, exfiltrating data, and issuing commands to infected devices. By targeting C2 infrastructure, defenders can disrupt the attacker's operations and isolate compromised systems.

- **C2 Disruption**: Small teams can use tools like **network monitoring**, **traffic analysis**, and **reverse engineering** of malware to locate and disrupt C2 servers. Once identified, defenders can block traffic to and from these servers, cutting off the attacker's ability to control compromised devices.
- **Decentralizing Defense**: As C2 servers are often single points of failure for attackers, disrupting them can render the entire attack ineffective. Small teams can use **decentralized defense strategies** to ensure that any disruptions to C2 infrastructure cause maximum damage to the attacker's operation.

3. EXPLOITING ATTACK TOOLS AND TECHNIQUES

Even the most sophisticated attackers rely on **specific tools** and **techniques** to execute their attacks. By analyzing these tools, small teams can develop **countermeasures** that neutralize the attacker's capabilities. For example, if attackers are using a specific malware strain, defenders can reverse-engineer the malware to understand its weaknesses and create **signatures** or **heuristic-based defenses** to block it.

- **Reverse Engineering Malware**: Once a piece of malware is identified, small teams can analyze its code, behavior, and communication patterns. This enables defenders to create customized defenses that block the malware's ability to function within the network.
- **Exploiting Malware Weaknesses**: Many malware strains contain coding errors, hardcoded credentials, or

dependencies that can be exploited by defenders. By identifying these weaknesses, small teams can prevent the malware from executing its intended actions or leverage the flaws to **track down** the attacker's infrastructure.

4. INFORMATION SHARING AND COLLABORATION

While small teams may lack the resources of larger organizations, they can amplify their defensive capabilities through **collaboration** and **information sharing**. By participating in threat intelligence networks, such as **Information Sharing and Analysis Centers (ISACs)**, defenders can gain access to real-time information on **new threats**, **attack patterns**, and **emerging vulnerabilities**. This collaboration allows small teams to **act quickly** and **proactively** before a threat escalates.

- **Leveraging Public-Private Partnerships**: Small teams can work closely with **national cybersecurity agencies, industry groups,** and other private sector partners to share intelligence on attacks. This collective defense strategy ensures that defenders have access to the latest information on evolving threats and can respond quickly.
- **Collective Defense**: When facing a sophisticated adversary like a nation-state, small teams can pool resources with other organizations to create a more robust defense. By collaborating with other cybersecurity teams, defenders can share insights, tools, and tactics to protect against large-scale attacks.

CASE STUDIES OF ASYMMETRIC CYBER DEFENSE AGAINST ADVANCED PERSISTENT THREATS (APTS)

To illustrate how small teams can successfully employ asymmetric tactics against larger threat actors, let's explore several **real-world**

case studies where small, agile teams effectively defended against **Advanced Persistent Threats (APTs)**.

1. OPERATION AURORA (2010)

Operation Aurora was a series of cyberattacks launched by a sophisticated APT group, believed to be backed by a nation-state, targeting major corporations such as **Google**, **Adobe**, and **Intel**. The attackers used **zero-day exploits** to gain access to sensitive intellectual property and corporate secrets.

- **Asymmetric Defense in Action**:
  Despite facing a well-funded, highly organized adversary, the security teams at Google employed **asymmetric tactics** to defend against the attack by Google's public disclosure and collaborative approach, which was quite unconventional at the time. As Google quickly identifying the malware used in the breach and conducting a **thorough forensic analysis**, the team was able to trace the attack back to the **command-and-control servers** used by the attackers. This information was shared with law enforcement and industry partners, leading to a **global effort** to disrupt the attacker's infrastructure and prevent further breaches.

2. TARGET DATA BREACH (2013)

In 2013, the American retail giant Target suffered a massive data breach that exposed the credit and debit card information of over 40 million customers. The breach occurred after attackers gained access through a third-party HVAC vendor, which allowed them to install malware on Target's point-of-sale (POS) systems.

- **Asymmetric Defense in Action**:
  In response to the breach, Target overhauled its cybersecurity strategy by investing heavily in **network segmentation** and advanced threat detection systems. The company worked with leading cybersecurity firms to deploy **advanced monitoring tools** capable of detecting anomalous behavior across its network. Target also adopted **asymmetric tactics,** such as implementing **whitelisting** and employing

behavioral analysis to identify potential insider threats and malware before they could cause damage. These new measures helped strengthen Target's defenses and significantly reduced the likelihood of a similar attack in the future.

-

3. CLOUDHOPPER ATTACKS (2014–2017)

The Cloudhopper attacks, attributed to the APT10 group, targeted managed service providers (MSPs) around the world from 2014 to 2017. These attacks allowed the hackers to infiltrate the networks of MSPs and subsequently gain access to the networks of their clients, stealing intellectual property and sensitive information from organizations across multiple industries.

- **Asymmetric Defense in Action**:
  To counter the Cloudhopper attacks, several MSPs and affected companies adopted asymmetric defense techniques, focusing on **multi-layered security** strategies. **Threat intelligence sharing** became a key component, as affected companies collaborated with international cybersecurity firms and government agencies to better understand the attackers' tactics. By utilizing **behavioral monitoring** and **deception technologies**, such as **honey tokens** (fake credentials or data designed to bait attackers), security teams were able to detect and analyze APT10's activities. This approach helped defenders stay ahead of the attackers, creating a more adaptive and proactive defense mechanism.

Conclusion: Asymmetry as a Force Multiplier for Small Teams

Asymmetric tactics provide small, agile cyber defense teams with a powerful set of strategies to defend against **nation-state attackers**, **organized crime**, and **advanced persistent threats**. By focusing on **speed, agility, deception**, and **targeted defenses**, small teams can exploit the weaknesses of larger adversaries, neutralizing their technological and resource advantages.

In today's cyber conflict landscape, where **APTs** and **sophisticated attackers** often hold the upper hand, asymmetry allows defenders to turn the tide. Whether by leveraging **SDN, AI, cyber deception**, or **collaborative defense**, small teams can remain agile, proactive, and resilient, ensuring that they stay one step ahead of even the most formidable adversaries.

CHAPTER 5: CYBER AMBUSH: SETTING TRAPS AND LURING ATTACKERS

INTRODUCTION

In traditional guerrilla warfare, the **ambush** is one of the most effective tactics used to surprise and overwhelm a stronger enemy. The essence of an ambush lies in **preparation, deception**, and **surprise**. Guerrilla fighters carefully plan their attack by identifying strategic locations where they can lay traps, then lure the enemy into these positions before launching a sudden strike. The enemy, caught off guard and outmaneuvered, is left with limited options, often leading to chaos and defeat.

In the digital world, the concept of ambush can be equally powerful. **Cyber ambush tactics** allow defenders to turn the tables on attackers by creating deceptive environments that lure adversaries into **traps**—giving defenders valuable time to gather intelligence, disrupt operations, and neutralize threats. By setting up decoys, honeypots, and dynamically reconfiguring networks, defenders can create a **layered defense** that keeps attackers off balance and forces them to waste resources on non-critical systems.

In this chapter, we will explore the **art of ambush in guerrilla warfare**, how it translates into the realm of **cyber defense**, and how modern technologies such as **Software Defined Networking (SDN)** and **Artificial Intelligence (AI)** can be leveraged to create real-time cyber ambushes. We will also discuss the **psychological impact** these tactics have on attackers, causing confusion, frustration, and a loss of confidence in their operations.

The Art of Ambush in Guerrilla Warfare

In traditional guerrilla warfare, ambushes are carefully planned attacks that rely on **surprise, preparation,** and **deception** to outmaneuver a larger or more powerful adversary. Ambushes typically involve selecting a location where the enemy is **vulnerable**—such as narrow terrain, a choke point, or an area where they are forced to travel. Guerrilla fighters **set traps**, wait for the enemy to approach, and then strike suddenly, exploiting the element of surprise to achieve a tactical victory.

KEY PRINCIPLES OF AMBUSH IN GUERRILLA WARFARE

1. **Choosing the Right Location**:
   The success of an ambush depends on selecting the right terrain. Guerrilla forces often choose locations that are advantageous to them and restrict the enemy's ability to maneuver, such as narrow passes, bridges, or dense forests.
2. **Deception and Misdirection**:
   Guerrilla fighters use **deception** to lure the enemy into the ambush site. This can involve creating false trails, using decoys, or deliberately retreating to draw the enemy into a vulnerable position.
3. **Surprise and Timing**:
   The effectiveness of an ambush lies in the element of **surprise**. Guerrilla fighters wait patiently, allowing the enemy to walk into the trap before launching their attack. Timing is critical—too early, and the enemy can retreat; too late, and the advantage is lost.
4. **Disruption and Confusion**:
   Ambushes are designed to cause maximum **disruption and**

confusion within the enemy ranks. By striking at the right moment, guerrilla fighters force the enemy into disarray, making it difficult for them to organize a counterattack.

The ambush tactic allows smaller forces to inflict disproportionate damage on a larger enemy by exploiting their **overconfidence** and **predictability**. In the context of cyber defense, these same principles can be used to set cyber ambushes that deceive attackers, waste their resources, and collect intelligence about their methods.

Setting Up Cyber Ambushes: Honeypots, Honeynets, and Decoys

In the world of **cybersecurity**, ambushes are typically executed through **deception techniques** designed to lure attackers into engaging with false systems, often called **honeypots, honeynets**, or **decoys**. These traps serve multiple purposes: they **distract** attackers from real assets, **gather intelligence** on their tactics and tools, and provide defenders with early warning of an intrusion.

1. HONEYPOTS

A **honeypot** is a decoy system that mimics a legitimate asset, such as a server, database, or network device. Honeypots are designed to appear vulnerable, inviting attackers to interact with them. Once an attacker engages with a honeypot, the system logs every action, command, and payload, allowing defenders to analyze the attacker's methods without risking the security of real systems.

- **Low-Interaction Honeypots**:
  These honeypots simulate the behavior of a vulnerable system but provide limited interaction for the attacker. They are primarily used for early detection of automated scanning tools or less sophisticated attackers. Their main purpose is to identify and flag potential threats.

- **High-Interaction Honeypots**:
  These honeypots closely mimic real systems, offering a full range of interaction to attackers. High-interaction honeypots are more useful for gathering detailed intelligence about advanced attackers. They simulate real operating systems and services, allowing attackers to spend more time interacting with the system, thus revealing more about their tools and objectives.

2. HONEYNETS

A **honeynet** is a network of honeypots, designed to simulate a complex environment. Honeynets are more advanced than individual honeypots because they mimic entire infrastructures, complete with servers, firewalls, databases, and other critical systems. This complexity makes them more appealing to sophisticated attackers who are looking to compromise a larger system or launch lateral movement within a network.

- **Research and Intelligence Gathering**:
  Honeynets are valuable for **researching attacker behavior** and **gathering intelligence** on APT groups or organized cybercrime syndicates. Because they simulate real networks, attackers are likely to deploy their most advanced tactics, techniques, and procedures (TTPs), which can be captured and analyzed by defenders.
- **Long-Term Engagement**:
  Honeynets are designed for **long-term engagement**, allowing attackers to spend significant time in the environment while defenders monitor their activities. This extended interaction provides defenders with insights into the attacker's objectives, infrastructure, and attack methodologies.

3. DECOY SYSTEMS

Decoy systems are fake systems or data assets designed to mislead attackers. Unlike honeypots, which are standalone systems, decoys are usually placed within real networks to create the appearance of high-value targets. These can include false databases, fake credentials, or misleading file structures.

- **Decoy Credentials**:
  Defenders can place **false credentials** in areas where attackers are likely to search, such as compromised machines or easily accessible files. When attackers use these credentials, they reveal their presence and allow defenders to track their movements.
- **Decoy Data and Files**:
  Fake files containing what appears to be sensitive information, such as financial data or intellectual property, can be placed in key areas. When attackers attempt to exfiltrate or tamper with this data, they trigger alerts, allowing defenders to respond before real data is compromised.

Setting up cyber ambushes using honeypots, honeynets, and decoys turns the attacker's own strategies against them. Instead of focusing solely on defending the perimeter, defenders can lure attackers deeper into the network, where they are isolated, monitored, and neutralized without compromising critical assets.

Dynamic Network Segmentation and Traffic Rerouting to Trap Attackers

In addition to using honeypots and decoys, cyber ambush tactics can be significantly enhanced through **dynamic network segmentation** and **traffic rerouting**. These tactics make it harder for attackers to move laterally through a network, while also allowing defenders to steer malicious traffic into ambush zones or decoy environments.

1. DYNAMIC NETWORK SEGMENTATION

Traditional networks are often static, with fixed segments and limited ability to adjust to emerging threats. However, **dynamic network segmentation**, enabled by technologies such as **SDN**, allows defenders to continuously reconfigure the network based on real-time threats. By dynamically segmenting the network, defenders can **isolate attackers** in specific zones and prevent them from accessing critical systems.

- **Micro-Segmentation:**
  Micro-segmentation is a technique that divides the network into small, isolated segments. Each segment is independently controlled and monitored, ensuring that even if an attacker compromises one part of the network, they cannot easily move laterally to other segments. This limits the scope of the attack and forces the attacker to spend more time navigating the network—giving defenders more opportunities to detect and contain the intrusion.

- **Dynamic Access Control:**
  With dynamic network segmentation, access controls can be adjusted in real-time based on user behavior or detected threats. If an attacker is identified in one segment of the network, access controls in that area can be tightened, while legitimate users are rerouted to unaffected segments.

2. TRAFFIC REROUTING TO AMBUSH ZONES

Traffic rerouting is a powerful tool for trapping attackers. Once malicious activity is detected, defenders can use SDN to **reroute traffic** away from critical systems and into decoy environments or honeypots. This serves two purposes: it protects real systems from further compromise and traps the attacker in an environment where their actions can be monitored.

- **Rerouting Suspicious Traffic:**
  If suspicious traffic or behavior is detected, SDN can be used

to **dynamically reroute** this traffic into a **honeypot** or **ambush zone**. The attacker, believing they are moving deeper into the network, is actually engaging with a decoy system designed to track their activities.
- **Isolating Compromised Systems**:
When a system is compromised, defenders can reroute all incoming and outgoing traffic for that system into a **sandboxed environment** where the attacker's movements can be observed in isolation. This containment strategy prevents the attacker from accessing other systems while giving defenders time to assess the situation and respond.

Dynamic network segmentation and traffic rerouting transform the network into an active defense mechanism that can **adapt** and **respond** to threats in real-time. These tactics not only limit the impact of an attack but also provide opportunities for defenders to turn the tables on the attacker.

Leveraging SDN and AI for Real-Time Ambush Tactics

To execute **real-time cyber ambush tactics**, defenders must rely on advanced technologies such as **Software Defined Networking (SDN)** and **Artificial Intelligence (AI)**. These tools provide the speed, flexibility, and automation necessary to set and trigger ambushes at a moment's notice, while also analyzing attacker behavior in real-time.

1. Software Defined Networking (SDN)

SDN decouples the control plane from the data plane in a network, allowing defenders to centrally manage and **reconfigure network traffic** in real-time. SDN is critical for setting ambushes because it allows defenders to create **dynamic network environments** that can be adjusted based on the attacker's movements.

- **Real-Time Reconfiguration:**
  With SDN, defenders can instantly **reconfigure network segments**, isolate compromised systems, or reroute traffic into decoy environments. This dynamic capability allows defenders to set traps and adjust the network topology on the fly, making it difficult for attackers to navigate.
- **Creating Ambush Zones:**
  SDN can be used to create **ambush zones**—specific areas of the network that are designed to lure attackers in. Once an attacker enters the ambush zone, SDN can block their access to the rest of the network and reroute all traffic to **honeypots** or **honeynets**. This isolates the attacker while keeping critical systems safe.

2. ARTIFICIAL INTELLIGENCE (AI)

AI plays a key role in detecting **anomalous behavior**, predicting attacker movements, and triggering ambush tactics in real-time. AI-powered systems can analyze vast amounts of network data, identifying suspicious patterns that indicate an attacker's presence.

- **Anomaly Detection:**
  AI-driven systems use **machine learning algorithms** to detect deviations from normal user behavior or network traffic. When an anomaly is detected, the system can trigger ambush tactics, such as rerouting traffic or deploying decoy systems.
- **Predictive Analytics:**
  AI can use **predictive analytics** to anticipate an attacker's next move. By analyzing past attack patterns and current behavior, AI systems can predict which systems the attacker is likely to target next, allowing defenders to preemptively set up ambushes in those areas.
- **Automated Response:**
  Once an ambush is triggered, AI systems can automatically execute **response actions**, such as isolating compromised systems, blocking malicious IP addresses, or adjusting access

controls. This automation ensures that defenders can respond to threats in real-time without manual intervention.

By leveraging SDN and AI, defenders can create **adaptive, real-time cyber ambush tactics** that are capable of outmaneuvering even the most sophisticated attackers.

Psychological Impact of Ambush Tactics on Attackers

Beyond the technical advantages, **cyber ambush tactics** can have a profound **psychological impact** on attackers. Just as ambushes in traditional warfare are designed to **disorient** and **demoralize** the enemy, cyber ambushes can cause attackers to lose confidence in their operations, second-guess their methods, and ultimately abandon their attacks.

1. Confusion and Disorientation

When attackers encounter honeypots, decoys, or rerouted traffic, they may become **confused** and **disoriented**, unsure whether they are interacting with a real system or a trap. This uncertainty forces them to spend more time analyzing their surroundings, slowing down their attack and giving defenders more time to respond.

- **Wasting Resources**:
  Attackers may waste significant resources—time, effort, and tools—engaging with decoy systems. By the time they realize they have been trapped, they may have already revealed critical information about their methods and infrastructure.

2. Frustration and Abandonment

Cyber ambush tactics can also lead to **frustration** on the part of the attacker. When attackers realize they have been deceived or lured into a trap, they may lose confidence in their ability to successfully complete the attack. This frustration can lead them to **abandon the operation** altogether or take more reckless actions, making them easier to detect.

- **Misdirection**:
  By consistently misdirecting attackers with decoys and traps, defenders can create an environment where the attacker no longer trusts their own intelligence. This erodes the attacker's confidence and increases the likelihood that they will make mistakes.

3. PSYCHOLOGICAL DETERRENCE

The knowledge that a network is equipped with **ambush tactics** can act as a **psychological deterrent** to future attacks. If attackers know that they are likely to encounter honeypots, decoys, and dynamic defenses, they may be less willing to risk an attack, fearing that they will be caught or misled.

- **Erosion of Trust**:
  Cyber ambush tactics erode the **trust** that attackers have in their own reconnaissance efforts. If they cannot distinguish between real assets and decoys, they are more likely to hesitate, second-guess their actions, and ultimately abandon the attack.

Conclusion: Cyber Ambush as a Strategic Tool

The art of the **cyber ambush** is a powerful strategy in modern cyber defense, allowing defenders to **turn the tables** on attackers by setting traps, luring them into vulnerable positions, and neutralizing their operations before critical systems are compromised. By using tools such as **honeypots, honeynets,** and **decoy systems**, combined with **dynamic network segmentation** and **traffic rerouting**, defenders can create **layered defenses** that keep attackers off balance.

With technologies like **SDN** and **AI**, defenders can take cyber ambush tactics to the next level, creating **real-time adaptive defenses** that respond instantly to threats and outmaneuver attackers. Beyond the technical advantages, cyber ambush tactics also have a profound **psychological impact** on attackers, causing confusion, frustration, and ultimately leading to the **failure of their operations.**

In the following chapters, we will explore how these ambush tactics can be integrated with **offensive cyber capabilities** to create a proactive defense strategy that not only disrupts attacks but also strikes back against adversaries, neutralizing their ability to launch future attacks.

CHAPTER 6: CYBER DECEPTION AND MISINFORMATION AS A STRATEGIC DEFENSE

INTRODUCTION

In the realm of **cyberwarfare**, traditional defenses such as firewalls, intrusion detection systems, and antivirus software, though necessary, are often insufficient when faced with sophisticated attackers like **Advanced Persistent Threats (APTs)** or **organized cybercrime syndicates.** These attackers can evade detection, bypass perimeter defenses, and infiltrate even the most secure networks. To stay ahead, defenders must employ more **proactive** and **unconventional** strategies, and one of the most effective among these is **cyber deception.**

Deception has long been a core element of **guerrilla warfare**, where smaller, less-resourced forces use tactics such as **misinformation, decoys,** and **ambushes** to disorient and outmaneuver a stronger enemy. In cyberspace, these same principles can be applied to create environments that **confuse, mislead, and frustrate attackers**, forcing them to waste resources on false targets while defenders gather valuable intelligence. **Cyber deception** uses fake systems, data, and even personas to manipulate attackers into revealing their methods and objectives, allowing defenders to gain the upper hand.

In this chapter, we will explore the **role of deception in traditional guerrilla warfare**, how it can be translated into the digital domain, and the tools and technologies—such as AI—that make cyber deception a potent strategy for modern cyber defense. We will also review **case studies** on plausible cyber deception operations that have thwarted attackers and protected critical infrastructure.

The Role of Deception in Traditional Guerrilla Warfare

In **traditional guerrilla warfare**, deception is used to **mislead** and **confuse** the enemy, forcing them to make mistakes, overextend themselves, or act on false information. Guerrilla fighters, often outnumbered and outgunned, use deception as a way to create **asymmetry**—allowing them to strike at the enemy's weak points while avoiding direct confrontation.

KEY PRINCIPLES OF DECEPTION IN GUERRILLA WARFARE

1. **Feints and False Retreats**:
   Guerrilla forces often use **feints**—fake attacks or retreats—to lure the enemy into a vulnerable position. By making it appear as though they are retreating or weakening, guerrilla fighters can draw the enemy into an **ambush** or into territory where the defenders have the advantage.
2. **Misinformation and Disinformation**:
   Misinformation involves feeding the enemy **false intelligence** that leads them to make poor decisions. This could involve leaking false plans, providing misleading intelligence about troop movements, or planting false information about the strength of forces. Disinformation, in particular, is designed to **erode the enemy's confidence** and **cause confusion**.

3. **Decoys and False Targets**:
   Decoy tactics involve creating **fake assets** or **false targets** that divert the enemy's attention away from the real objectives. These decoys can take the form of fake military outposts, false communication signals, or misleading supply lines, all designed to force the enemy to waste time and resources attacking something of no real value.
4. **Camouflage and Concealment**:
   Guerrilla fighters also use **camouflage** to conceal their real positions or intentions. By blending into the environment or making their forces appear smaller or less significant than they are, guerrilla fighters can **mislead** the enemy about the true nature of their operations.

In guerrilla warfare, deception is not just about misleading the enemy; it is about creating opportunities to exploit the enemy's weaknesses. By confusing and demoralizing the enemy, guerrilla forces can weaken their resolve and force them into mistakes. In **cyber defense**, these same principles can be applied to create deceptive environments that trick attackers into revealing their methods, wasting their resources, and losing their tactical advantage.

How Misinformation and Deception Disorient Attackers

In **cyberwarfare**, attackers often operate under the assumption that they can **reconnoiter** a network, **identify weak points**, and **move laterally** through systems without much resistance. They rely on gaining **situational awareness**—a clear understanding of the network's structure, defenses, and vulnerabilities—before launching an attack. Cyber deception, however, seeks to disrupt this process by **disorienting attackers** and preventing them from gaining a clear picture of the environment.

1. DISRUPTING RECONNAISSANCE EFFORTS

Reconnaissance is often the first step in a cyberattack, where attackers attempt to map out the network, identify vulnerable systems, and gather intelligence on security measures. **Deceptive environments** thwart this effort by **feeding false data** back to the attacker, making it impossible for them to distinguish between real and fake systems.

- **Fake Vulnerabilities**:
  Deception techniques can involve creating **fake vulnerabilities**—systems or services that appear to be weak but are actually decoys. When attackers attempt to exploit these vulnerabilities, they are drawn deeper into the deceptive environment, wasting time and resources.
- **Bogus Network Topologies**:
  Attackers rely on network mapping tools to create a visual representation of the target's infrastructure. By **feeding fake network data** to these tools, defenders can make it appear as though the network is much larger, more complex, or configured differently than it actually is. This causes attackers to misallocate their resources and misinterpret their progress.

2. CREATING UNCERTAINTY AND FORCING MISTAKES

Attackers, especially those involved in **Advanced Persistent Threats (APTs)**, are often highly methodical in their approach. They carefully plan their moves, taking steps to avoid detection and maintain persistence within the network. By using cyber deception, defenders can introduce **uncertainty** into the attacker's operations, forcing them to question every move they make.

- **Misleading Alerts and Logs**:
  By manipulating **system logs** and **alerts**, defenders can make it appear as though attackers are under constant surveillance or that their actions have triggered critical alerts. This causes

attackers to second-guess their methods and either slow down or abandon their operations.
- **Disinformation Campaigns:**
Defenders can feed **disinformation** to attackers by planting fake data or issuing false responses. For example, attackers may be led to believe they have successfully exfiltrated valuable data, only to realize later that the data is useless. This type of **data poisoning** can severely disrupt an attacker's plans, as they waste time analyzing and verifying the authenticity of their stolen information.

3. OVERLOADING ATTACKERS WITH FALSE DATA

Cyber deception tactics can overwhelm attackers by creating a flood of **false data** and **decoy systems** that force them to waste time analyzing dead ends. When every system could be a trap and every piece of data could be fake, attackers are left with little actionable intelligence, making it difficult for them to make progress.

- **Decoy Credentials and Files:**
Attackers often search for **credentials** or **sensitive files** to gain access to more critical systems. By planting **decoy credentials** or **false files**, defenders can lead attackers down the wrong path, causing them to waste valuable time while exposing their methods to defenders.
- **Multiple Layers of Deception:**
Deceptive environments can be **layered**, with multiple honeypots, fake systems, and false data scattered throughout the network. As attackers navigate through these layers, they become increasingly frustrated, unsure which systems are real and which are decoys. This increases the likelihood that they will make mistakes, such as triggering alerts or revealing their tactics.

Creating Fake Systems and Data to Mislead Adversaries

One of the most effective ways to implement cyber deception is by creating **fake systems** and **data assets** that appear to be legitimate but are designed solely to mislead attackers. These fake systems—often referred to as **honeypots, honeynets,** or **decoy systems**—are integral to deception strategies, as they provide attackers with attractive but ultimately useless targets.

1. Honeypots and Honeynets

As discussed in Chapter 5, **honeypots** and **honeynets** are decoy systems designed to simulate real assets and lure attackers into engaging with them. These systems appear to be part of the organization's infrastructure but are actually isolated and monitored by defenders.

- **Simulating Vulnerabilities**:
  Honeypots often simulate **vulnerable services** or **exploitable systems** to attract attackers. These vulnerabilities could be outdated software versions, misconfigured servers, or open ports that attackers typically look for. Once attackers engage with the honeypot, their activities are logged, allowing defenders to analyze their techniques.
- **Creating Honeynets**:
  A **honeynet** extends the concept of a honeypot by creating an entire network of decoy systems. Honeynets mimic the organization's real infrastructure, complete with fake databases, servers, and communication channels. Attackers who attempt lateral movement within the honeynet are essentially navigating a false environment, while defenders observe their every move.

2. DECOY SYSTEMS AND DATA

In addition to honeypots, defenders can create **decoy systems** that blend seamlessly into the real network. These decoy systems are designed to mimic high-value assets, such as **file servers, databases,** or **cloud storage systems**, tricking attackers into thinking they have found a valuable target.

- **Decoy Credentials and User Accounts:**
  Attackers often look for **compromised user accounts** or stolen credentials to move laterally through the network. By planting **decoy credentials** in known breach locations or compromised devices, defenders can monitor how attackers use these credentials to move through the network.
- **Fake Databases and Files:**
  Decoy databases can be populated with **fake data**, such as fabricated financial records, false customer information, or misleading intellectual property. When attackers exfiltrate this data, they believe they have successfully stolen valuable information, but in reality, the data is worthless. This not only wastes the attacker's resources but also creates opportunities for defenders to trace how the data is used or transmitted.

3. DYNAMIC DECOY SYSTEMS

One of the key challenges in cyber deception is ensuring that the decoy systems remain believable over time. Attackers often monitor networks for long periods, and static decoys may eventually be detected. To address this, defenders can deploy **dynamic decoy systems** that adjust and evolve in response to attacker behavior.

- **Rotating Decoy Assets:**
  By **rotating** decoy systems and periodically changing the configuration of honeypots, defenders can ensure that attackers are continuously interacting with fresh, believable

targets. This makes it harder for attackers to identify decoys over time.
- **Decoy Network Traffic**:
Decoy systems can also generate **fake network traffic** that mimics the behavior of real users or systems. This further enhances the believability of the decoy environment, as attackers see what appears to be legitimate activity within the fake system.

AI's Role in Deploying and Managing Deceptive Systems

Artificial Intelligence (AI) plays a critical role in the deployment and management of **cyber deception** systems. AI-driven deception tools can dynamically create and adjust decoys in real-time, respond to attacker behavior, and ensure that deceptive environments remain convincing over the course of an attack. AI also helps reduce the manual workload required to maintain these systems, allowing defenders to focus on higher-level strategy and decision-making.

1. Dynamic Decoy Deployment

AI can be used to **dynamically deploy decoy systems** based on real-time analysis of network activity. Instead of manually configuring honeypots or decoy systems, AI systems can automatically create and adjust these environments in response to emerging threats.

- **Automated Honeypot Creation**:
AI-driven systems can automatically create honeypots that are customized to the attacker's behavior. For example, if an attacker is targeting specific vulnerabilities or services, the AI can deploy honeypots that simulate those vulnerabilities, increasing the likelihood that the attacker will engage with the decoy.
- **Adaptive Deception**:
As attackers interact with decoy systems, AI can adjust the

environment in real-time to maintain the illusion. For instance, if an attacker attempts to move laterally from one decoy system to another, the AI can generate additional fake assets or modify existing ones to keep the attacker engaged.

2. BEHAVIORAL ANALYSIS AND THREAT DETECTION

AI is also critical for analyzing attacker behavior within deceptive environments. By monitoring how attackers interact with honeypots, honeynets, or decoy systems, AI can identify **patterns, techniques, and objectives**, allowing defenders to gain deeper insights into the attacker's strategy.

- **Behavioral Monitoring**:
  AI systems can monitor an attacker's actions within a decoy environment, analyzing everything from the commands they execute to the data they attempt to access. This provides valuable intelligence on the attacker's methods and objectives.
- **Predictive Analytics**:
  By analyzing past attack patterns, AI can use **predictive analytics** to anticipate an attacker's next move. For example, if an attacker has attempted to exploit certain vulnerabilities, the AI can predict which systems they are likely to target next and adjust the deception environment accordingly.

3. AUTOMATION AND ORCHESTRATION

One of the key advantages of AI in cyber deception is its ability to **automate** and **orchestrate** complex deception environments. AI-driven tools can manage multiple layers of deception, deploying and rotating decoy systems, generating fake traffic, and ensuring that the entire environment remains believable over time.

- **Orchestration of Decoy Networks**:
  AI systems can orchestrate entire decoy networks, ensuring that fake systems, data, and traffic are seamlessly integrated

into the real network. This makes it harder for attackers to distinguish between real and fake assets, increasing the likelihood that they will fall into the trap.
- **Automated Response and Escalation**:
When an attacker interacts with a decoy system, AI can automatically escalate the response based on the severity of the threat. For example, if an attacker attempts to move laterally, AI can isolate the compromised system, deploy additional decoys, or alert human operators for further investigation.

CASE STUDIES ON PLAUSIBLE CYBER DECEPTION OPERATIONS

Several real-world cyber deception operations are plausible and can demonstrated the effectiveness of using fake systems, data, and misinformation to **thwart attacks** and **gather intelligence**. These case studies highlight how deception can turn the tide in cyber conflict by forcing attackers to reveal their methods and waste resources on false targets.

1. OPERATION SMOKE SCREEN: DECEPTION AGAINST APT GROUPS

A major financial institution targeted by an **Advanced Persistent Threat (APT)** group attempting to exfiltrate sensitive customer data. The institution's cybersecurity team deployed a network of **honeypots** and **decoy systems** designed to mimic critical financial servers.

- **Deception Tactics Used**:
The APT group, believing they had gained access to a valuable server, spent weeks attempting to extract customer data from the decoy system. Meanwhile, the defenders collected detailed information about the group's tools, techniques, and command-and-control infrastructure.

- **Outcome**:
  By the time the APT group realized they had been deceived, the defenders had already reported the group's infrastructure to law enforcement, leading to the shutdown of the attacker's C2 servers. The financial institution's real assets remained untouched, and the attackers were forced to abandon their campaign.

2. THE MIRAGE INCIDENT: DECOY DATA AS A COUNTERMEASURE

A major aerospace company suspecting it was being targeted by cyber espionage agents seeking to steal proprietary designs for a new aircraft. In response, the company's security team deployed a series of **decoy databases** containing fake design plans.

- **Deception Tactics Used**:
  The attackers, believing they had successfully breached the company's internal network, exfiltrated large quantities of fake data. For weeks, the attackers analyzed the decoy designs, only to discover later that the data was useless.
- **Outcome**:
  The attackers' efforts were rendered futile, and the real design plans remained secure. The company was able to trace the attackers' network infrastructure and shared this intelligence with global partners, leading to the identification of the cyber espionage group.

Conclusion: Cyber Deception as a Strategic Defense

Cyber deception is one of the most powerful tools in the defender's arsenal. By creating **fake systems, decoy data,** and **misleading environments,** defenders can **disorient attackers,** force them to reveal their methods, and gain valuable intelligence while protecting real assets. The principles of deception in traditional guerrilla warfare—**misdirection, false targets,** and **camouflage**—translate directly into cyberspace, allowing defenders to outmaneuver more powerful adversaries.

The integration of **AI** and **dynamic decoy systems** makes cyber deception even more effective, allowing defenders to **automate** and **orchestrate** complex deception environments that adapt in real-time to attacker behavior. As seen in several real-world cases, cyber deception can lead to **successful defense** against even the most sophisticated attackers, forcing them to waste resources, make mistakes, and ultimately abandon their operations.

CHAPTER 7: PROACTIVE THREAT HUNTING AND INTELLIGENCE SHARING

Introduction

As cyber threats become increasingly sophisticated and frequent, organizations must shift their defensive posture from a **reactive** approach—waiting for attacks to occur—to a **proactive** one, where threats are actively sought out and mitigated before they can cause damage. This shift is essential for defending against **Advanced Persistent Threats (APTs), nation-state attacks, and cybercriminal organizations**, all of which possess the time, resources, and expertise to evade traditional, static defenses. **Proactive threat hunting** and **real-time intelligence sharing** are critical elements of a modern cybersecurity strategy, enabling defenders to anticipate and neutralize threats while also benefiting from collective defense efforts across industries and national borders.

In this chapter, we will explore the **importance of proactive defense**, the role of **Artificial Intelligence (AI)** in **real-time threat detection and analysis**, how **Software Defined Networking (SDN)** can be leveraged for **dynamic threat mitigation**, and the value of **collaborating with allies** and **sharing intelligence** to strengthen mutual defense. By adopting a proactive mindset and harnessing advanced technologies, organizations can stay ahead of attackers and build more resilient cyber defenses.

The Need for Proactive Defense

Traditional cybersecurity strategies have long relied on **reactive defenses**, where security teams respond to threats after they have been detected. This approach worked well when most attacks were opportunistic and unsophisticated, with attackers relying on known vulnerabilities and mass-distributed malware. However, as the threat landscape has evolved, reactive defenses have proven insufficient against **targeted attacks, zero-day exploits**, and **stealthy infiltration tactics** used by APTs and nation-state attackers.

1. REACTIVE DEFENSE: THE CHALLENGES

In a reactive defense model, organizations often rely on **firewalls, antivirus software**, and **intrusion detection systems (IDS)** to detect threats and raise alerts after malicious activity has already begun. While these tools are essential, they are limited in their ability to detect new or evolving threats. By the time a breach is detected, the attacker may have already gained access to critical systems, exfiltrated data, or disrupted operations.

- **Delayed Detection**:
  Reactive defenses often rely on **signature-based detection**, which only identifies known threats. This means that **zero-day attacks** or custom-built malware can go undetected for long periods, giving attackers ample time to achieve their objectives.
- **Post-Breach Response**:
  In a reactive defense model, the focus is on **responding to breaches** rather than preventing them. While organizations may have strong incident response plans, the fact remains

that they are dealing with the aftermath of an attack, rather than stopping it before damage occurs.
- **Overwhelming Alerts:**
  Security teams often face an overwhelming volume of **false positives** from traditional detection systems, making it difficult to prioritize real threats. This creates **alert fatigue**, where genuine threats may be missed amid a flood of benign alerts.

2. THE SHIFT TO PROACTIVE DEFENSE

To counter these challenges, organizations are increasingly adopting a **proactive defense posture**, where the focus is on **anticipating and neutralizing threats** before they can materialize. Proactive defense involves actively searching for threats—both inside and outside the network—through techniques such as **threat hunting, continuous monitoring**, and **real-time analysis**.

- **Threat Hunting:**
  Proactive threat hunting is a practice where security teams actively search for signs of compromise within the network, even if no alerts have been triggered. This approach relies on **anomaly detection**, behavioral analysis, and expert knowledge to identify **early indicators of compromise** (IoCs) that may not be flagged by automated systems.
- **Real-Time Threat Intelligence:**
  Proactive defense also involves leveraging **real-time threat intelligence** from internal sources (such as logs, user behavior analytics, and network traffic) as well as external feeds (such as industry-specific threat intelligence platforms). By staying informed about emerging threats, organizations can adjust their defenses accordingly.
- **Predictive Analytics:**
  Using technologies such as **machine learning (ML)** and **predictive analytics**, security teams can identify **patterns** in network behavior that suggest an impending attack. These insights enable organizations to preemptively deploy

countermeasures, such as updating access controls, patching vulnerabilities, or rerouting traffic.

By adopting a **proactive defense strategy**, organizations can **mitigate risks** before they escalate, reducing the likelihood of data breaches, system compromises, and operational disruptions.

AI's Role in Real-Time Threat Detection and Analysis

The increasing complexity and speed of cyberattacks make it impossible for human defenders to manually analyze all network traffic, logs, and potential indicators of compromise. This is where **Artificial Intelligence (AI)** and **machine learning** come into play. AI can significantly enhance a security team's ability to detect, analyze, and respond to threats in real-time, ensuring that even the most subtle indicators of malicious activity are identified and addressed.

1. AI-POWERED THREAT DETECTION

AI-powered systems can analyze vast amounts of data in real-time, detecting **anomalies** and **patterns** that suggest malicious activity. Traditional security systems rely on **predefined rules** or **signatures** to detect threats, making them effective only against known attacks. AI, however, can learn to identify abnormal behavior without relying on predefined signatures, making it highly effective at detecting **zero-day exploits, fileless malware**, and **advanced persistent threats**.

- **Anomaly Detection**:
  AI systems can continuously monitor network traffic, user behavior, and system activities, identifying deviations from the norm that may indicate a security incident. For example, if a user who typically logs in from a single device at a specific time suddenly begins accessing the network from multiple devices in different locations, AI systems can flag this as suspicious and trigger further investigation.

- **Behavioral Analytics**:
  AI-driven **behavioral analytics** allow organizations to establish a baseline of normal user and system behavior. When deviations occur—such as unusual login times, large data transfers, or unexpected application usage—AI can raise alerts for further scrutiny.
- **Threat Intelligence Integration**:
  AI can also integrate with **threat intelligence feeds** to cross-reference internal activity with known external threats. For example, if malicious IP addresses, phishing domains, or malware signatures are identified in external threat feeds, AI can correlate this information with internal network traffic to detect potential compromises.

2. MACHINE LEARNING FOR THREAT ANALYSIS

Machine learning (ML) is a subset of AI that focuses on enabling systems to learn from data and improve their performance over time. In cybersecurity, ML models can be trained on historical attack data to recognize patterns associated with known threats, while also learning to identify new attack vectors based on subtle changes in behavior.

- **Learning from Historical Data**:
  ML systems are trained on large datasets of both benign and malicious network traffic, enabling them to differentiate between normal and abnormal behavior. As they process more data, these systems continuously refine their models, improving their ability to detect **emerging threats**.
- **Predicting Future Attacks**:
  In addition to detecting current threats, ML can be used for **predictive analytics**—anticipating future attacks based on observed patterns and trends. For example, if an attacker is conducting **reconnaissance** by scanning for open ports or probing for vulnerabilities, ML algorithms can predict which systems or services are likely to be targeted next, enabling defenders to proactively secure those assets.

- **Automated Threat Response**:
  Once a threat is detected, AI can automate the **response process**, such as **isolating compromised systems, blocking malicious IP addresses**, or **revoking access privileges**. This rapid response capability is critical for preventing attackers from gaining a foothold or moving laterally within the network.

AI's ability to **analyze massive amounts of data in real-time**, detect anomalies, and predict future attacks makes it an indispensable tool in the **proactive defense** strategy.

USING SDN FOR DYNAMIC THREAT MITIGATION

Software Defined Networking (SDN) is a critical technology for enabling **dynamic threat mitigation** in real-time. SDN decouples the **control plane** from the **data plane**, allowing network administrators to centrally control network traffic and make changes dynamically. This flexibility is key to mitigating threats quickly, isolating compromised systems, and adjusting network configurations in response to evolving attacks.

1. DYNAMIC NETWORK RECONFIGURATION

In a traditional network, reconfiguring the infrastructure to respond to a threat is a slow and manual process, often requiring changes to individual devices such as routers, switches, and firewalls. **SDN** streamlines this process by enabling **centralized control** over the entire network, allowing defenders to **reconfigure the network in real-time**.

- **Quarantine and Isolation**:
  When malicious activity is detected, SDN allows defenders to instantly **quarantine compromised systems** by creating isolated segments within the network. This prevents

attackers from moving laterally and accessing more critical systems. For example, if a workstation is suspected of being compromised, SDN can automatically reroute traffic away from that device and limit its access to sensitive resources.

- **Dynamic Traffic Rerouting**:
  In the event of a **Distributed Denial of Service (DDoS)** attack, SDN can dynamically **reroute network traffic** to mitigate the impact of the attack. By distributing traffic across multiple paths or redirecting it to scrubbing centers, SDN minimizes the disruption caused by the attack and ensures that legitimate traffic continues to flow.

2. MICRO-SEGMENTATION FOR THREAT CONTAINMENT

Micro-segmentation is an advanced security practice that involves dividing the network into smaller, isolated segments, each with its own set of security policies. This approach limits the attack surface by preventing unauthorized lateral movement within the network. **SDN** enables the implementation of **real-time micro-segmentation**, allowing defenders to dynamically adjust the size, scope, and security policies of each segment in response to detected threats.

- **Granular Access Control**:
  Micro-segmentation allows for **granular control** over which users, devices, and applications can communicate with each other. For example, in the event of an attack, access to critical systems can be restricted to only the most trusted users and devices, while all other connections are blocked or rerouted.
- **Automatic Policy Enforcement**:
  SDN makes it possible to **automatically enforce security policies** across the network. For instance, if an anomaly is detected in one segment of the network, SDN can automatically adjust the security policies for that segment, such as increasing the logging level, applying additional firewalls, or restricting certain types of traffic.

3. THREAT INTELLIGENCE-DRIVEN RESPONSES

By integrating **real-time threat intelligence** with **SDN**, organizations can enable automated, intelligence-driven responses to emerging threats. For example, if external threat intelligence identifies a specific IP address or domain associated with a known attack campaign, SDN can automatically **block traffic** from that source, preventing the attack from reaching the network.

- **Proactive Blocking**:
  SDN can proactively **block traffic** from known malicious IP addresses, domains, or regions based on real-time threat intelligence feeds. This prevents attackers from initiating communication with compromised systems or conducting reconnaissance.
- **Dynamic Network Adjustments**:
  When threat intelligence indicates a surge in attack activity (e.g., a wave of phishing emails or ransomware attacks targeting a specific industry), SDN can dynamically adjust network configurations to protect vulnerable systems, such as implementing additional firewalls, increasing authentication requirements, or isolating high-value assets.

By leveraging **SDN** for **dynamic threat mitigation**, organizations can respond to attacks faster, contain threats more effectively, and minimize the impact of security incidents.

COLLABORATING WITH ALLIES AND SHARING INTELLIGENCE FOR MUTUAL DEFENSE

Cybersecurity is not a battle that can be fought in isolation. Today's cyber threats are global, sophisticated, and often coordinated by highly organized adversaries. To stay ahead of these threats, organizations must engage in **collaborative defense**—sharing **threat intelligence** with industry peers, government agencies, and international coalitions. **Intelligence sharing** enables defenders to stay informed about the latest attack methods, vulnerabilities, and indicators of compromise, while also contributing to the collective security of the broader community.

1. THE VALUE OF INTELLIGENCE SHARING

Threat intelligence sharing provides organizations with real-time information about **emerging threats, attack vectors**, and **malicious actors**. By pooling resources and sharing insights, organizations can **detect attacks earlier, mitigate risks more effectively**, and prevent **widespread damage**.

- **Real-Time Threat Feeds**:
  Participating in **threat intelligence sharing platforms** provides access to real-time threat feeds that include **malicious IP addresses, domains, file hashes**, and **IoCs** associated with known attacks. This information helps organizations block or mitigate threats before they reach their networks.
- **Crowdsourced Insights**:
  In addition to technical indicators, intelligence sharing platforms provide **crowdsourced insights** from other organizations that have experienced similar attacks. These insights can include details on attacker tactics, techniques, and procedures (TTPs), as well as lessons learned from previous incidents.

2. INFORMATION SHARING AND ANALYSIS CENTERS (ISACS)

Information Sharing and Analysis Centers (ISACs) are industry-specific organizations designed to facilitate collaboration and intelligence sharing among companies within the same sector. For example, there are ISACs for finance, healthcare, energy, and transportation. By participating in ISACs, organizations can stay informed about threats that are specific to their industry and receive tailored guidance on how to defend against those threats.

- **Sector-Specific Threats**:
  Each industry faces unique threats based on the nature of its operations. For example, the financial sector may be targeted by **ransomware** and **financial fraud**, while the energy sector may face **nation-state attacks** on critical infrastructure. ISACs provide sector-specific threat intelligence that is directly relevant to the organization's risk profile.
- **Incident Response Coordination**:
  ISACs also facilitate **incident response coordination** in the event of a large-scale cyberattack. By working together, organizations can share resources, expertise, and intelligence to contain and mitigate the impact of the attack.

3. PUBLIC-PRIVATE PARTNERSHIPS

Public-private partnerships are critical for enhancing national and global cybersecurity. Governments, through agencies such as **national cybersecurity centers**, often have access to classified intelligence, threat assessments, and law enforcement resources that can be invaluable to private sector organizations. By collaborating with government agencies, organizations can access **early warnings** about nation-state threats, critical vulnerabilities, and ongoing attack campaigns.

- **Law Enforcement Collaboration**:
  In cases of cybercrime, collaboration with **law enforcement agencies** can help trace attackers, disrupt their infrastructure, and bring perpetrators to justice. For example, organizations that are targeted by ransomware can work with law enforcement to track cryptocurrency payments, identify the ransomware operators, and recover stolen data.
- **Government Threat Sharing Platforms**:
  Many governments have established **threat intelligence sharing platforms** that provide real-time alerts and analysis to both public and private sector organizations. These

platforms enable organizations to stay informed about nation-state threats, cyber espionage campaigns, and other critical cybersecurity risks.

4. INTERNATIONAL CYBER DEFENSE COALITIONS

In an increasingly interconnected world, cyber threats often transcend national borders. **International cyber defense coalitions**, such as the **Global Forum on Cyber Expertise (GFCE) and NATO's Cooperative Cyber Defence Centre of Excellence (CCDCOE),** promote cross-border collaboration, intelligence sharing, and capacity building to enhance global cybersecurity resilience.

- **Cross-Border Threat Intelligence**:
  International coalitions facilitate the sharing of threat intelligence across borders, ensuring that organizations in different countries can collaborate on detecting and mitigating global threats. For example, if a nation-state attack is detected in one country, intelligence about the attack can be shared with international partners to prevent the attack from spreading.
- **Cyber Defense Exercises**:
  Many international coalitions conduct **cyber defense exercises**, where member countries simulate large-scale cyberattacks and practice coordinated responses. These exercises help improve the collective readiness of the global cybersecurity community to respond to major incidents.

Conclusion: The Power of Proactive Defense and Intelligence Sharing

The **cyber threat landscape** is constantly evolving, with attackers becoming more sophisticated, stealthy, and persistent. To defend against these threats, organizations must adopt a **proactive defense** strategy—one that actively seeks out and neutralizes threats before they can cause damage. **Proactive threat hunting**, powered by **AI** and **real-time threat intelligence**, enables defenders to anticipate attacks and stay one step ahead of adversaries.

By leveraging technologies such as **SDN** for **dynamic threat mitigation**, organizations can rapidly isolate compromised systems, reroute traffic, and adjust security policies to contain attacks in real-time. Moreover, **collaborating with allies** and engaging in **intelligence sharing** are critical to strengthening mutual defense efforts. Whether through **ISACs**, **public-private partnerships**, or **international coalitions**, intelligence sharing ensures that defenders can collectively respond to emerging threats and prevent widespread cyberattacks.

CHAPTER 8: ZERO TRUST ARCHITECTURE AND DYNAMIC ACCESS CONTROL

Introduction

As cyberattacks become increasingly sophisticated, organizations are recognizing that traditional security models—based on the assumption that everything inside the network perimeter is trusted—are no longer effective. The rise of **insider threats**, **lateral movement** by attackers, and the erosion of network boundaries due to cloud adoption and remote work have highlighted the need for a new approach to cybersecurity. This is where the **Zero Trust Architecture (ZTA)** comes into play.

Zero Trust is a security model that assumes no user, device, or system can be trusted by default, regardless of whether they are inside or outside the network perimeter. Instead, trust is established **continuously** based on identity, context, and behavior, with access granted only on a **need-to-know basis**. This philosophy ensures that even if an attacker gains access to the network, they are prevented from moving laterally or accessing critical systems without going through strict verification processes.

In this chapter, we will explore the fundamentals of **Zero Trust**, why it is critical for modern cybersecurity, and how **AI-driven continuous authentication** and **Software Defined Networking (SDN)** can be used to implement and enhance Zero Trust principles. We will also examine how **micro-segmentation** and **guerrilla-style ambush tactics** can be applied to dynamically secure networks and limit the impact of breaches.

THE ZERO TRUST PHILOSOPHY AND WHY IT'S CRITICAL

The traditional approach to network security has been based on the concept of a **secure perimeter**. Once users, devices, or applications gain access to the internal network, they are typically granted **implicit trust**, allowing them to interact freely with other systems and data within the network. However, this model has inherent weaknesses, as it fails to account for the possibility of **insider threats** or attackers who have successfully breached the perimeter.

1. THE WEAKNESSES OF PERIMETER-BASED SECURITY

The traditional perimeter-based security model is often referred to as the **"castle-and-moat"** approach, where firewalls and other perimeter defenses act as the moat, protecting the internal systems (the castle). While this model worked well when networks were more contained, it is increasingly inadequate in modern IT environments where:

- **Insider Threats**: Once inside the network, attackers—whether malicious insiders or external actors who have gained access—can move laterally with relative ease, compromising critical systems and exfiltrating data.

- **Remote Work and Cloud Environments**: The shift to **remote work** and **cloud adoption** has blurred the traditional network perimeter. Employees and devices now access corporate resources from various locations and devices, making it difficult to control and secure the network based solely on perimeter defenses.
- **Supply Chain and Third-Party Risks**: Organizations increasingly rely on third-party vendors, contractors, and supply chain partners who may have access to internal systems. This opens up new attack vectors that perimeter defenses are ill-equipped to manage.

2. THE CORE PRINCIPLES OF ZERO TRUST

In contrast to the perimeter-based model, **Zero Trust** operates on the principle of **"never trust, always verify."** No user, device, or application is trusted by default, even if they are already inside the network. Instead, access is **dynamically granted** based on a combination of factors, such as identity, device health, location, and behavioral context.

The core principles of Zero Trust include:

- **Least Privilege Access**: Users and devices are only given the minimum level of access necessary to perform their tasks. This minimizes the potential damage an attacker can cause if they gain access to the network.
- **Continuous Verification**: Access is **continuously verified** throughout the session, not just at the initial login. This ensures that even if a session is compromised, the attacker cannot continue to access systems undetected.
- **Micro-Segmentation**: The network is divided into smaller, isolated segments (or **zones**) with strict access controls. This limits the ability of attackers to move laterally across the network if they breach one segment.
- **Contextual Access Control**: Access decisions are made based on real-time context, such as the user's location, device

health, and behavior. If any anomalies are detected, access can be restricted or revoked immediately.
- **Assume Breach**: Zero Trust assumes that breaches will occur and builds defenses that limit the potential damage. By segmenting the network and verifying every access request, the model minimizes the attacker's ability to escalate their privileges or access sensitive data.

By enforcing these principles, Zero Trust ensures that **trust is never implicit** and that all access is **verified and contextually based**. This greatly reduces the risk of unauthorized access and helps contain attacks before they spread.

Implementing AI-Driven Continuous Authentication

One of the key challenges in implementing **Zero Trust** is the need for **continuous authentication**—the process of continually verifying the identity and legitimacy of users, devices, and applications throughout their sessions. Traditional authentication methods, such as **passwords** or **multi-factor authentication (MFA)**, are typically performed once at the beginning of a session and are not repeated unless there is an explicit reason to re-authenticate. This leaves a security gap if a session is compromised.

1. THE LIMITATIONS OF TRADITIONAL AUTHENTICATION

Traditional authentication methods have several limitations that make them ill-suited for Zero Trust environments:

- **One-Time Verification**: In traditional models, authentication typically occurs once at the start of a session. After the user is authenticated, they are granted access to resources for the duration of the session, with no further verification. This creates a risk if an attacker takes control of the session after authentication has occurred.

- **Static Authentication Factors**: While MFA is an improvement over password-only authentication, it still relies on static factors, such as passwords, one-time codes, or biometrics, which can be compromised or stolen. MFA, by itself, is not enough to provide continuous protection throughout the session.

2. AI-DRIVEN CONTINUOUS AUTHENTICATION

Artificial Intelligence (AI) can address these limitations by enabling **continuous authentication**, where user behavior and context are continuously analyzed throughout the session to verify identity and detect anomalies. AI-driven systems can assess a wide range of factors to ensure that access remains secure, even if an attacker gains access to the user's credentials.

- **Behavioral Biometrics**: AI systems can monitor **behavioral biometrics**—such as typing patterns, mouse movements, and touchscreen gestures—to establish a baseline of normal user behavior. If an attacker takes over a session, deviations in these patterns can be detected, and the system can trigger re-authentication or session termination.
- **Contextual Analysis**: AI can also analyze **contextual factors** in real-time, such as the user's location, device health, and network conditions. For example, if a user logs in from one geographic location and then attempts to access sensitive data from another location shortly afterward, AI systems can flag this as suspicious and request additional verification.
- **Risk-Based Authentication**: AI-driven authentication systems can implement **risk-based** or **adaptive authentication**, where access decisions are dynamically adjusted based on the assessed risk level. Low-risk activities, such as viewing non-sensitive data, may not require additional authentication, while high-risk activities, such as accessing financial systems, may trigger re-authentication.
- **Automated Incident Response**: If an AI system detects suspicious activity, such as an anomaly in user behavior, it

can automatically initiate **incident response actions**, such as requiring MFA, logging out the user, or isolating the affected system for further investigation.

AI-driven continuous authentication provides the **dynamic verification** needed to secure access in a Zero Trust environment. By analyzing a wide range of factors in real-time, AI can detect and respond to potential threats before they escalate, ensuring that **trust is continuously reassessed** throughout the session.

USING SDN TO ENFORCE MICRO-SEGMENTATION AND LIMIT LATERAL MOVEMENT

One of the most critical elements of **Zero Trust Architecture (ZTA)** is **micro-segmentation**, which involves dividing the network into smaller, isolated segments, each with its own set of access controls and security policies. **Software Defined Networking (SDN)** is a key technology for implementing and managing micro-segmentation, as it allows for **centralized control** over the network and enables real-time adjustments to security policies.

1. THE IMPORTANCE OF MICRO-SEGMENTATION IN ZERO TRUST

Micro-segmentation limits an attacker's ability to move laterally through the network by **restricting access** between different segments. This is essential in a Zero Trust environment, where the goal is to minimize the impact of a breach by **containing the attacker** in a single segment and preventing them from reaching critical assets.

- **Lateral Movement**: Once an attacker gains access to a network, their next objective is typically to move laterally—gaining access to additional systems, escalating privileges, and ultimately reaching sensitive data or critical infrastructure. In a flat, unsegmented network, this lateral

movement is often easy to achieve, as there are few internal barriers to stop them.
- **Isolated Zones**: Micro-segmentation creates **isolated zones** within the network, each with its own set of access controls. For example, the finance department's systems may be isolated from the HR department's systems, and access between the two zones is strictly controlled. If an attacker compromises a system in one zone, they cannot easily move to other zones without going through additional verification.

2. SDN-ENABLED MICRO-SEGMENTATION

Software Defined Networking (SDN) enables **dynamic micro-segmentation**, allowing network administrators to centrally control and adjust network segments in real-time based on security needs. SDN decouples the **control plane** from the **data plane**, providing a centralized view of the entire network and making it easier to enforce **fine-grained access controls** between different segments.

- **Dynamic Access Control**: With SDN, access controls can be **dynamically adjusted** based on real-time threat intelligence, user behavior, and network conditions. For example, if an anomaly is detected in one segment of the network, SDN can automatically restrict access to that segment, preventing attackers from moving laterally to other parts of the network.
- **Automated Threat Containment**: SDN can also be used to **automatically isolate** compromised systems or segments of the network. If malicious activity is detected in one zone, SDN can quickly reroute traffic, block communication between segments, or apply additional security policies to contain the threat.
- **Centralized Policy Management**: SDN provides a **centralized platform** for managing security policies across the entire network. This makes it easier to enforce consistent security policies across different segments and quickly respond to emerging threats by adjusting access controls or rerouting traffic.

By using SDN to implement micro-segmentation, organizations can **limit lateral movement**, contain threats more effectively, and ensure that access to sensitive systems is tightly controlled.

Adopting Guerrilla-Style Ambush Tactics Through Network Segmentation

In traditional guerrilla warfare, **ambush tactics** involve setting traps for the enemy, luring them into vulnerable positions, and then striking when they least expect it. These principles can be applied to **cyber defense** by using **network segmentation** to create **ambush zones**—areas of the network that are designed to **trap attackers** and prevent them from reaching critical systems.

1. CREATING AMBUSH ZONES WITH SEGMENTATION

In a Zero Trust environment, network segmentation can be used to create **ambush zones** that appear to be high-value targets but are actually **decoy systems** or **honeypots**. When an attacker attempts to move laterally into one of these zones, they are funneled into a controlled environment where their actions can be monitored and contained.

- **Deceptive Segmentation**: Defenders can use segmentation to create **decoy zones** that mimic the appearance of critical systems, such as financial databases or administrative servers. These zones are isolated from the real systems and designed to lure attackers into engaging with fake data or vulnerable-looking services.
- **Monitoring and Intelligence Gathering**: Once an attacker enters an ambush zone, their actions can be closely monitored, allowing defenders to gather valuable intelligence about their methods, tools, and objectives. This intelligence can be used to strengthen defenses and respond more effectively to future attacks.

2. LEVERAGING SDN FOR AMBUSH TACTICS

SDN plays a key role in enabling **dynamic ambush tactics** by allowing defenders to **reconfigure the network** in real-time and funnel attackers into controlled environments. With SDN, network administrators can quickly create or adjust ambush zones based on real-time threat intelligence and attacker behavior.

- **Real-Time Rerouting**: If malicious activity is detected, SDN can be used to **reroute traffic** away from critical systems and into ambush zones. This ensures that attackers are contained in a safe environment where their actions can be monitored without risking the integrity of real systems.
- **Dynamic Deception**: SDN can also enable **dynamic deception**, where decoy zones are continuously adjusted to keep attackers off balance. By periodically rotating decoy systems, changing network configurations, and introducing new ambush zones, defenders can make it difficult for attackers to map the network or identify real targets.

3. PSYCHOLOGICAL IMPACT OF AMBUSH TACTICS

Ambush tactics not only contain attackers but also have a significant **psychological impact**. When attackers realize they have been trapped in an ambush zone, they may become **confused** or **frustrated**, leading them to make mistakes or abandon the attack entirely.

- **Wasting Attacker Resources**: By luring attackers into decoy zones, defenders can **waste the attacker's time and resources**, forcing them to expend effort on systems that have no real value. This not only disrupts the attack but also reduces the likelihood of a successful breach.
- **Eroding Attacker Confidence**: Ambush tactics can also **erode the attacker's confidence** in their ability to navigate the network. When attackers are repeatedly misled or trapped in decoy systems, they may lose trust in their own

reconnaissance and question whether they can continue the attack effectively.

By adopting **guerrilla-style ambush tactics** through network segmentation, defenders can turn the tables on attackers, using deception and dynamic reconfiguration to **confuse, contain,** and **neutralize threats** before they reach critical systems.

Conclusion: Zero Trust Architecture and Dynamic Access Control as the Future of Cyber Defense

The rise of **advanced cyber threats**, the breakdown of traditional network perimeters, and the increasing reliance on cloud services and remote work have made **Zero Trust Architecture (ZTA)** a critical component of modern cybersecurity. By assuming that no user, device, or system can be trusted by default, Zero Trust ensures that access to sensitive resources is **continuously verified** and based on **contextual factors** such as identity, behavior, and risk.

AI-driven continuous authentication and **SDN-enabled micro-segmentation** are key enablers of Zero Trust, providing the real-time intelligence and control needed to secure dynamic environments. By leveraging these technologies, organizations can **limit lateral movement, contain threats,** and enforce **fine-grained access controls** that minimize the potential damage of a breach.

Moreover, by adopting **guerrilla-style ambush tactics** through network segmentation, defenders can use deception and dynamic reconfiguration to **trap attackers**, gather intelligence, and disrupt attacks before they escalate. This proactive, adaptive approach to security ensures that even the most sophisticated attackers are **contained and neutralized** before they can cause significant harm.

CHAPTER 9: RESILIENT INFRASTRUCTURE AND REDUNDANCY IN A DYNAMIC ENVIRONMENT

Introduction

In today's rapidly evolving threat landscape, having a **resilient network architecture** is critical for ensuring the continuity of business operations in the face of cyberattacks, natural disasters, and system failures. Resilience in network architecture means the ability to **withstand, adapt to**, and **recover from** disruptions while minimizing the impact on critical systems and services. With the rise of **nation-state attackers, advanced persistent threats (APTs)**, and increasingly sophisticated ransomware, organizations must not only secure their networks but also ensure that their infrastructure is **resilient** enough to recover quickly from any kind of disruption.

To achieve this, organizations are leveraging technologies like **Software Defined Networking (SDN)** and **Artificial Intelligence (AI)** to build **dynamic infrastructures** that can rapidly respond to incidents. These technologies enable **real-time reconfiguration, automated recovery**, and **hit-and-run mobility tactics**, ensuring that data and services remain available even in the face of persistent attacks.

This chapter will explore how to build a **resilient network architecture**, the role of **SDN** in enabling **rapid reconfiguration and traffic rerouting**, how AI supports **automated backup and recovery**, and how adopting **mobility** as a defensive strategy can prevent attackers from gaining a foothold in the network.

Building a Resilient Network Architecture

A **resilient network architecture** is designed to **withstand disruptions**, whether they are caused by cyberattacks, hardware failures, or natural disasters. Resilience is about ensuring that **critical services remain available** and **data integrity** is maintained, even when parts of the infrastructure are compromised. Achieving this requires a combination of **redundancy, fault tolerance,** and **real-time monitoring**.

1. KEY COMPONENTS OF A RESILIENT ARCHITECTURE

A resilient network architecture consists of several key components, each of which contributes to the overall ability to **prevent, detect,** and **recover** from disruptions.

- **Redundancy**:
  Redundancy involves creating **duplicate systems** or **backup resources** that can take over if the primary system fails. This includes having redundant network connections, power supplies, and backup servers. Redundancy is crucial for ensuring **high availability**, as it provides a fallback option if the primary infrastructure is compromised.
- **Fault Tolerance**:
  Fault-tolerant systems are designed to continue operating even when some components fail. This can be achieved through techniques like **distributed computing**, where multiple nodes share the workload, and the system can continue functioning even if one node goes down. Fault tolerance also extends to **storage systems**, where **data replication** ensures that a copy of critical data is always available in case of hardware failure.
- **Load Balancing**:
  Load balancing distributes network traffic across multiple servers to ensure that no single server is overwhelmed. This not only improves performance but also provides resilience against **Denial of Service (DoS)** attacks. If one server is compromised or taken offline, traffic can be redirected to other servers without affecting the availability of services.
- **Disaster Recovery Planning**:
  A resilient network architecture must include a **disaster**

recovery plan (DRP) that outlines how the organization will respond to and recover from major disruptions. This plan should cover everything from **data recovery** to **rebuilding infrastructure** and should be regularly tested through **disaster recovery exercises**.
- **Geographic Distribution**:
In the age of **cloud computing** and **global business operations**, geographic distribution is critical for resilience. Data centers and cloud services should be **distributed across multiple geographic locations**, ensuring that if one location experiences an outage or attack, services can continue from another site.

2. THE IMPORTANCE OF FLEXIBILITY AND ADAPTABILITY

Building a resilient network architecture is not just about having redundant systems; it's also about ensuring that the architecture is **flexible** and **adaptable**. In today's dynamic threat environment, attackers constantly evolve their techniques, so the network infrastructure must be capable of **adapting in real-time** to new threats.

- **Dynamic Resource Allocation**:
One of the keys to flexibility is **dynamic resource allocation**, where computing and network resources can be adjusted on the fly to respond to changing conditions. For example, during a DDoS attack, additional bandwidth can be allocated to absorb the traffic, or during a surge in legitimate traffic, load balancers can automatically allocate more servers to handle the demand.
- **Programmability**:
Modern network architectures are increasingly **software-driven**, meaning they can be reprogrammed in real-time to respond to incidents. This allows for **rapid changes** to network configurations, firewall rules, or access controls without requiring manual intervention.

By designing networks that are both **redundant** and **flexible**, organizations can ensure that their infrastructure remains operational even in the face of sophisticated and persistent cyberattacks.

USING SDN FOR RAPID RECONFIGURATION AND TRAFFIC REROUTING

Software Defined Networking (SDN) is a powerful tool for achieving network resilience through its ability to **rapidly reconfigure** network infrastructure and **reroute traffic** in response to incidents. SDN enables **centralized control** over the entire network, allowing administrators to **dynamically adjust** the flow of traffic, reallocate resources, and isolate compromised systems in real-time.

1. THE ROLE OF SDN IN DYNAMIC NETWORK MANAGEMENT

One of the key benefits of SDN is its ability to provide **real-time visibility** and **control** over the network, enabling organizations to respond quickly to threats or failures. With SDN, network administrators can **automate** many aspects of network management, reducing the time it takes to detect and mitigate disruptions.

- **Centralized Control Plane**:
  SDN separates the **control plane** from the **data plane**, allowing for centralized management of the network. This enables administrators to view and control the entire network from a single console, making it easier to respond to incidents and apply **security policies** across the network.
- **Real-Time Reconfiguration**:
  When a disruption occurs—whether due to an attack or a hardware failure—SDN allows for **instantaneous reconfiguration** of the network. For example, if a router fails, SDN can automatically reroute traffic through alternative paths, ensuring that services remain available. This real-time

reconfiguration is essential for **maintaining uptime** and **preventing bottlenecks** during incidents.
- **Automated Traffic Rerouting**:
  In the case of a **cyberattack** such as a **Distributed Denial of Service (DDoS)**, SDN can automatically reroute malicious traffic away from critical systems and toward **scrubbing centers** that filter out the malicious traffic. This allows legitimate traffic to continue flowing while minimizing the impact of the attack.

2. ENHANCING NETWORK RESILIENCE WITH SDN

SDN's ability to rapidly reconfigure the network makes it an ideal technology for enhancing **network resilience**. By dynamically adjusting the flow of traffic and reallocating resources, SDN ensures that the network remains operational even under duress.

- **Dynamic Segmentation**:
  SDN enables **dynamic segmentation** of the network, where different parts of the network can be isolated in response to security incidents. If a segment of the network is compromised, SDN can quarantine that segment while allowing other parts of the network to continue functioning normally. This minimizes the impact of a breach and prevents attackers from moving laterally.
- **Traffic Load Balancing**:
  SDN can be used to dynamically balance traffic across multiple servers and data centers, preventing any single point from becoming a bottleneck or failure point. This ensures that if one server goes down or is overwhelmed, traffic can be seamlessly redirected to other servers.
- **Programmable Security Policies**:
  SDN allows for **programmable security policies** that can be automatically adjusted in response to detected threats. For example, if an intrusion detection system (IDS) flags suspicious activity, SDN can immediately update firewall

rules, block malicious IP addresses, or reroute traffic through additional security checks.

By providing the ability to **rapidly reconfigure** and **dynamically adjust** network infrastructure, SDN plays a critical role in building a **resilient and adaptive network** capable of responding to a wide range of threats and disruptions.

The Role of AI in Automated Backup and Recovery Processes

In a resilient infrastructure, the ability to **quickly recover** from disruptions is just as important as the ability to **withstand** them. **Artificial Intelligence (AI)** is playing an increasingly important role in **automating backup** and **recovery processes**, ensuring that data can be restored and systems can be brought back online quickly after an incident.

1. Automated Data Backup and Integrity Checks

One of the primary uses of AI in resilient infrastructures is in **automating data backup** processes. Traditional backup systems often rely on manual scheduling and configuration, which can lead to errors or missed backups. AI-driven backup systems, on the other hand, can automatically adjust backup schedules based on **real-time data usage** and **storage availability**, ensuring that critical data is always backed up.

- **Dynamic Backup Scheduling**:
  AI can optimize backup schedules based on the importance of the data and its usage patterns. For example, AI systems can prioritize **mission-critical data** for more frequent backups while reducing the frequency for less critical data. This ensures that **key systems** can be restored quickly in the event of an outage or attack.

- **Data Integrity Verification**:
  AI can also automate the process of verifying **data integrity** by continuously monitoring backup systems for signs of corruption or failure. If an issue is detected, AI systems can trigger an immediate re-backup, ensuring that the organization always has a valid, uncorrupted copy of its critical data.

2. AI-DRIVEN RECOVERY PROCESSES

When a disruption occurs, speed is of the essence. AI-driven recovery systems can **automate** many of the tasks involved in bringing systems back online, reducing the time it takes to restore services and minimizing downtime.

- **Automated Failover Systems**:
  AI can be used to manage **automated failover systems**, where if one part of the infrastructure goes down, another part automatically takes over. For example, if a data center experiences an outage, AI-driven systems can automatically reroute workloads to a secondary data center, ensuring continuity of service.
- **Predictive Maintenance**:
  AI can predict when critical infrastructure components—such as servers, routers, or storage systems—are likely to fail, based on real-time monitoring of system performance and historical data. By identifying potential failures before they occur, AI can trigger **proactive maintenance**, reducing the likelihood of unexpected outages and improving overall resilience.

3. AI IN DISASTER RECOVERY PLANNING

AI is also playing a growing role in **disaster recovery planning** by simulating potential failure scenarios and identifying **optimal recovery strategies**. These simulations allow organizations to prepare for a wide range of incidents and ensure that their disaster recovery plans are robust and effective.

- **Scenario Analysis**:
  AI-driven scenario analysis allows organizations to simulate various **disaster scenarios**, such as cyberattacks, natural disasters, or hardware failures, and assess their impact on the infrastructure. By running these simulations, organizations can identify **vulnerabilities** in their disaster recovery plans and make adjustments to improve their resilience.
- **Automated Recovery Orchestration**:
  In the event of a disaster, AI can **orchestrate the recovery process**, automatically restoring data, reconfiguring systems, and bringing critical services back online. This reduces the need for manual intervention and speeds up the recovery process, ensuring that the organization can resume operations quickly.

AI's ability to **automate backup and recovery processes** significantly improves an organization's ability to recover from disruptions, ensuring that critical data and services can be restored quickly and efficiently.

MOBILITY AS A DEFENSIVE STRATEGY: HIT-AND-RUN TACTICS FOR DATA AND SERVICES

In the face of persistent threats, organizations are increasingly adopting **mobility** as a **defensive strategy**. By making **data** and **services** more **mobile**—constantly moving them across different locations or systems—organizations can implement **hit-and-run tactics** that prevent attackers from gaining a foothold or accessing valuable information.

1. THE CONCEPT OF HIT-AND-RUN TACTICS IN CYBER DEFENSE

In traditional guerrilla warfare, **hit-and-run tactics** involve striking quickly and then retreating before the enemy can respond. This principle can be applied to cyber defense, where **data** and **services** are frequently moved or reconfigured, making it difficult for attackers to locate and exploit them.

- **Data Mobility**:
  By frequently moving critical data between different locations—such as **cloud environments, on-premises systems**, and **offsite backups**—organizations can make it harder for attackers to target and exfiltrate sensitive information. Even if an attacker gains access to one location, they may find that the data they are looking for has already been moved to another location.

- **Service Mobility**:
  Similar to data mobility, **service mobility** involves moving critical applications and services between different environments to prevent attackers from gaining persistent access. For example, a web application can be moved between different cloud providers or data centers based on real-time threat intelligence, making it difficult for attackers to launch sustained attacks against a single target.

2. DYNAMIC WORKLOADS AND RESOURCE ALLOCATION

Mobility as a defensive strategy also involves **dynamic workloads** and **resource allocation**, where computing resources are continuously reallocated based on **demand** and **security needs**. This ensures that critical services remain operational while minimizing the attack surface.

- **Cloud Bursting**:
  Cloud bursting is a technique where workloads are automatically moved to cloud environments during periods of high demand or when local resources are compromised.

This not only improves performance but also adds an extra layer of **resilience** by distributing workloads across multiple environments.
- **Dynamic Service Deployment**:
Services can be **dynamically deployed** in different environments based on real-time threat intelligence. For example, if a certain region is experiencing a wave of cyberattacks, services can be temporarily moved to data centers in other regions, reducing the risk of being targeted.

3. DISTRIBUTING CRITICAL ASSETS

By **distributing critical assets**—both data and services—across multiple locations, organizations can reduce the risk of a single point of failure and make it harder for attackers to launch coordinated attacks.

- **Multi-Cloud Strategy**:
A **multi-cloud strategy** involves using multiple cloud providers to host different parts of an organization's infrastructure. This provides redundancy and ensures that even if one provider experiences an outage or attack, the organization can continue operating from other providers.
- **Data Fragmentation**:
Data fragmentation involves breaking critical data into smaller pieces and storing those pieces in different locations. Even if an attacker gains access to one location, they will only have access to a fragment of the data, making it difficult to reconstruct or exploit the information.

By adopting **mobility as a defensive strategy**, organizations can use **hit-and-run tactics** to keep their data and services **dynamic**, reducing the risk of sustained attacks and ensuring that critical assets remain secure.

Conclusion: Building Resilience in a Dynamic Cyber Environment

In today's **dynamic cyber environment**, building a resilient infrastructure is essential for ensuring that organizations can withstand, adapt to, and recover from a wide range of disruptions. **Resilience** is about more than just preventing attacks—it's about ensuring that critical services remain available and that data can be restored quickly, even in the face of sophisticated threats.

Technologies like **SDN** and **AI** play a critical role in building resilience by enabling **rapid reconfiguration**, **traffic rerouting**, **automated recovery**, and **dynamic mobility**. By leveraging these technologies, organizations can create **redundant**, **adaptive** infrastructures that are capable of responding to incidents in real-time and minimizing the impact of cyberattacks.

Additionally, adopting **mobility as a defensive strategy** allows organizations to use **hit-and-run tactics** to keep data and services dynamic, making it difficult for attackers to gain persistent access. By constantly moving and reconfiguring critical assets, organizations can stay one step ahead of attackers and ensure that their infrastructure remains resilient and secure.

Chapter 10: Psyops Cyber Deception and the Art of the Ambush

Introduction

In warfare, one of the most potent tools a defender can wield is **deception**. Throughout history, psychological operations (**Psyops**) have been used to mislead, confuse, and demoralize enemies, ensuring that adversaries are unable to predict or anticipate the defender's next move. This concept has been adapted to the cyber domain, where attackers often attempt to gain as much intelligence as possible before launching their final assault. By integrating **Psyops tactics** and **cyber deception** into cybersecurity, defenders can create an environment where the attacker is never quite sure what is real and what is not.

In **cyberwarfare**, ambush and deception tactics are powerful because they target not just the technical aspects of the attack but the psychology of the attacker. By sowing **uncertainty, doubt,** and **frustration**, defenders can force attackers into making mistakes, abandoning their objectives, or revealing valuable intelligence. This chapter will delve into how organizations can use **Psyops tactics** alongside advanced technologies like **Software Defined Networking (SDN)** and **Artificial Intelligence (AI)** to set ambushes, deceive attackers, and fortify access control systems.

Building a Resilient Network Architecture

Before implementing Psyops tactics, it's essential to establish a **resilient network architecture**—one that can both withstand attacks and enable **dynamic deception** and **ambush strategies**. A resilient network ensures that, even when under attack, critical services and data remain operational, providing the defender with enough control to deploy psychological and technical traps.

1. Fault Tolerance and Redundancy

A **resilient architecture** incorporates **redundancy** and **fault tolerance** to ensure the network's continuity even when parts of it are compromised. Key systems and data must remain operational, allowing the defenders to maintain control over the environment and set their traps.

- **Distributed Systems:**
  Implementing **distributed systems** ensures that critical

services are mirrored across multiple geographic regions or cloud environments. This allows defenders to reroute operations seamlessly in the event of an attack, confusing the attacker by maintaining operational capacity even under duress.
- **Automated Failover**:
Automated failover systems can instantly switch operations to backup systems when primary systems are disrupted, enabling rapid recovery and continued operations. This resilience is critical for deploying deceptive tactics that require maintaining access to operational resources.

2. DYNAMIC RECONFIGURATION AND ADAPTABILITY

In a Psyops framework, **adaptability** is crucial. The network must be **dynamic** enough to confuse attackers with constant changes in configuration and routing. A **static network** provides attackers with a predictable environment, making it easier for them to map and exploit weaknesses.

- **Rapid Network Reconfiguration**:
A resilient network architecture that supports **rapid reconfiguration** allows defenders to quickly adapt to ongoing attacks. For example, if an attacker compromises a segment of the network, defenders can quickly isolate that segment, reroute traffic, and deploy decoy systems to trap the attacker.
- **Programmable Infrastructure**:
By using programmable infrastructure such as **SDN**, defenders can adjust network traffic flows, access control lists (ACLs), and firewall rules dynamically. This not only helps contain attacks but also allows for the creation of **false trails** and **deceptive network topologies** that mislead attackers about the real structure of the network.

Using SDN for Rapid Reconfiguration and Traffic Rerouting

Software Defined Networking (SDN) plays a critical role in creating the flexibility needed for **cyber deception**. It enables defenders to **control traffic flows** in real-time, reroute malicious traffic into **ambush zones**, and maintain the appearance of normal operations while isolating compromised systems.

1. DYNAMIC TRAFFIC REROUTING FOR DECEPTION

With SDN, defenders can **dynamically reroute traffic** to guide attackers into **honeypots**, **decoy environments**, or other controlled spaces where their actions can be monitored and analyzed without compromising real systems.

- **Ambush Zones**:
  Attackers often expect to navigate a predictable network topology. By dynamically rerouting traffic and segmenting parts of the network, SDN can create **ambush zones**—areas of the network that appear to be high-value targets but are, in fact, traps. Attackers are lured into these zones and forced to interact with **decoy systems**, revealing their tactics and techniques.
- **False Network Topologies**:
  SDN enables defenders to create **false network topologies** that lead attackers down the wrong path. By rerouting traffic and configuring decoy systems to mimic critical infrastructure, attackers can be tricked into believing they have accessed sensitive systems when, in reality, they are interacting with controlled decoys.

2. ISOLATING AND CONTAINING THREATS

SDN allows for **real-time isolation** of compromised segments, preventing attackers from moving laterally within the network. By restricting access and rerouting traffic, SDN ensures that even if a part of the network is breached, attackers cannot easily spread their influence.

- **Micro-Segmentation**:
  Through **micro-segmentation**, SDN enables defenders to tightly control which devices, users, or applications can communicate within the network. If an attacker compromises one part of the network, they are contained within that segment and prevented from accessing critical assets in other zones.
- **Programmable Security Policies**:
  SDN enables **programmable security policies** that can change in response to detected threats. For example, if a threat is identified, SDN can automatically enforce stricter security policies in the affected segment, blocking the attacker's attempts to escalate privileges or move laterally.

By using SDN to **rapidly reconfigure the network**, defenders can deploy **Psyops tactics** that confuse and mislead attackers, guiding them into ambush zones where their actions can be monitored, analyzed, and neutralized.

PSYOPS TACTICS IN CYBERWARFARE

Psychological operations (Psyops) have been a staple of military strategy for centuries, focusing on influencing the perceptions, decision-making, and morale of adversaries. In **cyberwarfare**, these tactics translate into **deceptive measures** designed to sow confusion, uncertainty, and doubt in the minds of attackers. The goal is to undermine the attacker's confidence, waste their resources, and disrupt their decision-making process.

1. MISINFORMATION AND DECEPTION

One of the core tactics of Psyops is **misinformation**—providing attackers with **false intelligence** that leads them to make mistakes or miscalculate their next move. In the cyber domain, misinformation can take the form of **decoy systems, fake data,** and **deliberate vulnerabilities** that lure attackers into wasting time and effort.

- **Decoy Systems and Honeypots**:
  Honeypots are designed to appear as legitimate systems, but in reality, they are traps set to capture attackers' tactics, techniques, and procedures (TTPs). By deploying honeypots that mimic real servers or applications, defenders can deceive attackers into thinking they have breached critical systems when they have only interacted with decoys.
- **False Vulnerabilities**:
  Defenders can introduce **false vulnerabilities** into the network to lure attackers into exposing themselves. For example, a decoy system may appear to have an unpatched vulnerability that attackers will attempt to exploit. This creates an opportunity for defenders to monitor the attack, gather intelligence, and deploy countermeasures.

2. PSYCHOLOGICAL IMPACT ON ATTACKERS

The effectiveness of Psyops in cyber defense hinges on the **psychological impact** it has on attackers. By creating an environment of uncertainty and doubt, defenders can cause attackers to question their tactics, lose confidence in their progress, and make critical errors.

- **Eroding Confidence**:
  Attackers who encounter **false information** or **deceptive systems** may become increasingly unsure of their success. When attackers realize that they have been interacting with decoy systems, their confidence erodes, leading them to

question their understanding of the network and their ability to succeed.
- **Forcing Errors**:
  In the face of **frustration** and **uncertainty**, attackers are more likely to make mistakes—such as triggering security alerts or exposing their own infrastructure. By constantly shifting the environment, defenders can force attackers to act rashly, increasing the likelihood of detection.

Psyops tactics in cyberwarfare are not just about tricking the attacker—they are about **controlling the narrative** of the attack. By feeding attackers false intelligence and misleading them at every turn, defenders can shape the course of the attack and force the adversary into a weakened position.

Psyops in Access Control Management to Deceive

Access control is a critical part of network defense, ensuring that only authorized users can access sensitive systems and data. By integrating **Psyops tactics** into **access control management**, defenders can **deceive attackers** attempting to escalate privileges or gain unauthorized access.

1. DYNAMIC ACCESS CONTROLS

Dynamic access controls adjust **permissions** and **privileges** in real-time based on **user behavior, context,** and **threat intelligence**. In a Psyops framework, access controls can be manipulated to **mislead attackers**, creating the illusion of access while restricting real capabilities.

- **Illusory Privilege Escalation**:
  Attackers often attempt to escalate privileges to gain access to more sensitive systems. By deploying **illusory privilege escalation**, defenders can make it appear that the attacker

has successfully gained higher-level access, only to lead them into a controlled environment or decoy system. This tactic wastes the attacker's time and resources while preventing access to real systems.
- **Deceptive Authentication Systems:**
  Decoy authentication systems can be used to capture the credentials or behavior of attackers attempting to log in to high-value systems. When attackers believe they have successfully logged in, they are actually interacting with a controlled system that monitors their every move.

2. AI-DRIVEN ACCESS CONTROL ADJUSTMENTS

Artificial Intelligence (AI) can enhance the **dynamic nature of access controls**, enabling real-time adjustments based on detected anomalies or suspicious behavior. AI can be programmed to detect **unusual access patterns** and immediately deploy **Psyops tactics** to deceive the attacker.

- **Contextual Authentication:**
  AI-driven systems can analyze **contextual factors** such as location, device type, and behavioral biometrics to determine whether an access request is legitimate. If an attacker attempts to mimic a legitimate user, AI can trigger a **deceptive response**, such as redirecting the attacker to a decoy system or requiring additional authentication.
- **Automated Policy Changes:**
  When AI detects a suspicious access attempt, it can automatically adjust **access control policies**, limiting the attacker's ability to move laterally or escalate privileges. These changes can be applied in real-time, creating a **fluid access environment** that confuses attackers and prevents them from gaining traction.

By using Psyops tactics in access control management, defenders can create a **dynamic and deceptive environment** that keeps attackers guessing, preventing them from achieving their objectives while gathering intelligence on their behavior.

The Role of AI in Automated Backup and Recovery Processes

Artificial Intelligence (AI) plays a crucial role in **automating backup and recovery processes**, ensuring that even when attackers attempt to disrupt or destroy data, defenders can quickly restore systems and maintain operational continuity. In the context of Psyops, AI also enables **deceptive recovery strategies** that make it difficult for attackers to assess the effectiveness of their attacks.

1. AI-DRIVEN DATA BACKUP

AI can **optimize backup processes** by analyzing real-time data flows and ensuring that **critical data** is continuously backed up to **secure locations**. In the event of an attack, AI-driven systems can restore data quickly, ensuring that the attacker's impact is minimal.

- **Continuous Backup Monitoring**:
  AI systems continuously monitor the **health and integrity** of backup processes, automatically flagging any anomalies or failures. This ensures that defenders always have access to a valid, uncorrupted backup, even if an attack attempts to compromise the backup infrastructure.
- **Prioritizing Critical Data**:
  AI-driven systems can prioritize the backup of **mission-critical data** based on usage patterns and risk assessments. This ensures that the most important data is always backed up first, allowing for rapid recovery in the event of an incident.

2. DECEPTIVE RECOVERY STRATEGIES

In a Psyops context, AI can be used to implement **deceptive recovery strategies** that confuse attackers about the success of their efforts.

For example, AI systems can simulate **data corruption** or **system failure**, leading attackers to believe they have successfully compromised the network, only for defenders to restore operations quickly from a backup.

- **Simulated Downtime**:
  AI can orchestrate **simulated downtime** to mislead attackers into thinking their attack has been successful. During this simulated downtime, defenders can analyze the attacker's methods, implement countermeasures, and restore operations without the attacker's knowledge.
- **Selective Data Restoration**:
  AI can restore data selectively, prioritizing the restoration of **less critical systems** to mislead attackers about the true state of recovery. Attackers may believe they have successfully destroyed important data, only to realize later that the real data has been safely restored from a secure backup.

AI's ability to **automate backup and recovery processes** ensures that defenders can maintain operational continuity even in the face of sophisticated attacks, while also leveraging **deceptive recovery tactics** to further confuse and mislead attackers.

Mobility as a Defensive Strategy: Hit-and-Run Tactics for Data and Services

In the face of persistent threats, mobility can be employed as a **defensive strategy**, using **hit-and-run tactics** for **data** and **services**. These tactics involve moving critical assets between **different locations** or **systems** to prevent attackers from gaining a foothold or successfully targeting them.

1. MOBILE DATA AND SERVICE MOBILITY

By **constantly moving data** and **services** across different cloud environments, geographic locations, or backup systems, defenders can make it difficult for attackers to lock onto a single target. Even if attackers manage to compromise one location, the data or services they are after may have already moved elsewhere.

- **Dynamic Data Movement**:
  In a hit-and-run strategy, critical data is **dynamically moved** between secure locations, such as cloud services, local storage, or offsite backups. This prevents attackers from targeting a single location for data exfiltration or encryption.
- **Mobile Services**:
  Key services, such as web applications or critical business processes, can be moved across different infrastructure providers or geographic regions. This mobility ensures that even if one location is compromised or taken offline, the service continues to operate from another location, frustrating the attacker's efforts to disrupt operations.

2. DYNAMIC WORKLOAD ALLOCATION

Using **dynamic workload allocation**, services and resources are constantly reallocated based on real-time demand, security needs, or detected threats. This fluid approach makes it harder for attackers to predict where data or services will be at any given time.

- **Cloud Bursting**:
  Cloud bursting allows organizations to move workloads to cloud environments during periods of high demand or when local resources are compromised. By constantly moving workloads between different environments, defenders can keep attackers off balance, preventing them from establishing a persistent foothold.
- **Fragmentation of Critical Data**:
  Data can be **fragmented** and stored in different locations, so

even if attackers gain access to one part of the data, they do not have the complete dataset. This fragmentation adds an extra layer of security, making it harder for attackers to extract valuable information.

By adopting **hit-and-run tactics** for data and services, defenders can keep critical assets **mobile** and **dynamic**, ensuring that attackers are always one step behind and unable to execute a successful attack.

CONCLUSION: THE POWER OF CYBER DECEPTION AND PSYOPS IN CYBER DEFENSE

The integration of **Psyops tactics** and **cyber deception** into cybersecurity strategies provides defenders with a powerful tool for controlling the narrative of an attack. By using **deceptive systems, dynamic access controls,** and **AI-driven recovery processes,** defenders can mislead attackers, erode their confidence, and force them into making critical mistakes.

With technologies like **SDN** enabling **rapid reconfiguration** and **traffic rerouting,** and **mobility tactics** keeping critical data and services dynamic, organizations can turn the tables on attackers, creating a **resilient and adaptable defense**. The psychological impact of these tactics—confusing, frustrating, and demoralizing attackers—ensures that defenders maintain the upper hand in the face of even the most sophisticated threats.

CHAPTER 11: OFFENSIVE CYBER CAPABILITIES AND PREEMPTIVE STRIKES

Introduction

In the ever-evolving landscape of cyber threats, defense alone may not always be sufficient to protect critical systems and data. While traditional cybersecurity strategies focus on defending against attacks, many organizations and governments are exploring the use of **offensive cyber capabilities** as a means to **neutralize threats** before they can cause damage. Offensive cyber operations are not just about responding to an attack but proactively identifying, disrupting, and dismantling adversaries' capabilities.

Offensive cyber capabilities include a range of tactics, from **preemptive strikes** to **hack-back operations** where defenders retaliate against or neutralize an attacker's infrastructure. These proactive measures can help disrupt adversaries' operations, reduce their effectiveness, and deter future attacks. However, the use of offensive cyber tactics raises significant **legal and ethical concerns**, as well as the potential for unintended consequences.

This chapter will examine how offensive cyber operations can be used as a **strategic tool for defense**, the conditions under which **preemptive strikes** and **hack-back tactics** are appropriate, and how organizations can **exploit weaknesses in adversary infrastructures**. We will also discuss the **legal** and **ethical frameworks** that must be considered when engaging in offensive cyber operations.

Offensive Cyber Operations as a Strategic Tool for Defense

Offensive cyber operations involve the deliberate and proactive use of cyber capabilities to **disrupt, degrade, or destroy** an adversary's systems, networks, or operations. These tactics are increasingly viewed as a necessary component of a comprehensive cyber defense strategy, particularly when facing **nation-state actors**, **advanced persistent threats (APTs)**, and **cybercriminal organizations** with significant resources and capabilities.

1. PROACTIVE DEFENSE THROUGH OFFENSE

Offensive cyber operations can be an effective way to **preemptively weaken** adversaries before they can launch attacks. By taking the fight to the attacker, defenders can reduce the likelihood of being targeted or can degrade the adversary's ability to carry out sustained operations.

- **Disrupting Attack Campaigns**:
  Offensive operations can target the **command and control (C2) infrastructure** of cybercriminals and APTs, disrupting their ability to coordinate attacks. By taking down these infrastructures, defenders can prevent or at least delay the execution of an attack.
- **Neutralizing Threat Actors**:
  In cases where a specific threat actor is identified, offensive cyber tactics can be used to **neutralize** the threat by infiltrating their systems, planting **countermeasures** such as malware, or exfiltrating sensitive information that disrupts their operations.
- **Deterrence**:
  Offensive cyber operations can serve as a **deterrent** against future attacks. When attackers know that a targeted organization is capable of retaliating or launching **preemptive strikes**, they may be less likely to engage with that organization due to the potential risks to their own infrastructure.

2. TYPES OF OFFENSIVE CYBER OPERATIONS

There are several types of offensive cyber operations that organizations or governments can employ to protect their interests. These include:

- **Active Defense**:
  Active defense strategies involve **monitoring, tracking**, and, when necessary, **disrupting** ongoing attacks in real-time. This

may include activities such as redirecting or **spoofing malicious traffic**, feeding false data back to the attacker, or actively hunting down the source of an attack.
- **Counter-Offensive Operations:**
  In a counter-offensive operation, defenders retaliate against an attacker by exploiting vulnerabilities in the attacker's systems or networks. This can involve planting **malware**, deleting or corrupting data, or overloading adversary systems to degrade their operational capabilities.
- **Preemptive Strikes:**
  Preemptive strikes involve taking action against a potential attacker before they launch an attack. This requires detailed **intelligence gathering** and may involve exploiting known vulnerabilities in the adversary's infrastructure to disrupt their plans.

By integrating these offensive cyber operations into their overall security strategy, organizations can create a **proactive defense posture** that not only defends against attacks but also **actively reduces the threat** posed by adversaries.

Preemptive Strikes: When to Engage in Hack-Back Tactics

A **preemptive strike** refers to taking proactive action against an adversary when there is strong intelligence indicating an imminent attack. Similarly, **hack-back tactics**—where defenders actively retaliate against an attacker's infrastructure—are controversial but can be effective when used correctly. These tactics are part of the broader category of **active defense**, but their use comes with significant **legal**, **ethical**, and **strategic considerations**.

1. THE RATIONALE FOR PREEMPTIVE STRIKES

Preemptive strikes are often justified when an organization believes it is on the verge of being attacked and wishes to **neutralize the** threat before it can materialize. This proactive approach can prevent **devastating attacks**, such as **ransomware, data breaches**, or **sabotage** of critical infrastructure.

- **Imminent Threat**:
  Preemptive strikes are typically justified when there is **clear evidence** that an attack is imminent. For example, if threat intelligence indicates that a known adversary is preparing to deploy ransomware across the organization's network, launching a preemptive strike to disrupt the attacker's infrastructure may prevent the attack from succeeding.
- **Disabling the Attacker's Infrastructure**:
  In many cases, preemptive strikes focus on disabling the attacker's **command-and-control (C2) servers, malware distribution networks**, or other key components of their infrastructure. By disrupting these systems, the defender can neutralize the attacker's ability to coordinate or launch attacks.
- **Preventing Escalation**:
  Preemptive strikes can also prevent the escalation of an attack by **disrupting the attacker's operational capabilities**. For instance, an adversary might be in the early stages of infiltrating a network and gathering intelligence. A preemptive strike could involve neutralizing the adversary's foothold before they can escalate to data exfiltration or ransomware deployment.

2. HACK-BACK TACTICS: THE CONTROVERSY

Hack-back tactics, also known as **active retaliation**, involve launching a **counter-attack** against an adversary after being targeted. Hack-back tactics are highly controversial because they can blur the lines between defense and aggression and may lead to **escalation** or unintended consequences.

- **Attribution Challenges**:
  One of the primary challenges with hack-back tactics is

attribution—accurately identifying the source of the attack. Cyberattacks are often carried out through **proxy servers**, **botnets**, or **hacked machines**, making it difficult to trace the true origin of the attack. Engaging in hack-back tactics without reliable attribution risks retaliating against innocent parties.

- **Escalation Risk:**
  Hack-back operations can escalate tensions between the attacker and defender, potentially leading to **cyber escalation** or retaliation. An attacker, once targeted by a hack-back operation, may respond with an even more aggressive attack, leading to a cycle of escalation that could have broader implications.
- **Legal Implications:**
  In many jurisdictions, hack-back tactics are **illegal**, as they may violate laws related to unauthorized access to computer systems. Organizations considering hack-back must carefully weigh the legal risks and potential for **collateral damage**.

Despite the controversy, hack-back tactics may be considered in extreme cases where the stakes are high, and all other defense mechanisms have been exhausted. However, these tactics should be executed with caution and in compliance with applicable laws.

Exploiting Weaknesses in Adversary Infrastructures

One of the most effective forms of offensive cyber operations involves **exploiting weaknesses** in an adversary's infrastructure. Just as attackers look for vulnerabilities in their target's systems, defenders can turn the tables by identifying and exploiting vulnerabilities in the attacker's systems, networks, or tools.

1. IDENTIFYING AND EXPLOITING VULNERABILITIES

Every cybercriminal organization, nation-state actor, or APT has its own infrastructure, which often contains **vulnerabilities** that can be exploited. These weaknesses might include **poorly secured servers, outdated software, misconfigured firewalls,** or even **human error** in their operational practices.

- **Reconnaissance on Adversary Systems:**
  Offensive cyber operations often begin with **reconnaissance** of the adversary's infrastructure. By analyzing traffic patterns, scanning for open ports, and identifying unpatched systems, defenders can gather intelligence on where the attacker's weak points lie. This intelligence can then be used to launch targeted attacks designed to **disrupt their operations.**
- **Deploying Exploits:**
  Once vulnerabilities are identified, defenders can deploy **exploits** to gain access to the adversary's systems. This may involve compromising their C2 servers, disabling key services, or stealing information about their planned operations. The goal is to cause **disruption** and **degradation** of the attacker's ability to launch future attacks.

2. DISRUPTING MALWARE DEVELOPMENT AND DISTRIBUTION

Many cybercriminal groups rely on **malware** to carry out their operations. Offensive cyber operations can target the **malware development process,** infiltrating the attacker's development pipeline, or sabotaging malware distribution networks.

- **Sabotaging Malware Distribution:**
  Attackers often rely on **botnets** or **malware distribution networks** to spread their tools across the internet. By infiltrating these networks, defenders can sabotage the malware before it reaches its intended targets. This might

involve inserting **kill switches** into the malware, **redirecting traffic**, or corrupting the files to render them ineffective.
- **Corrupting Attackers' Tools**:
Offensive cyber operations can also target the **tools** that attackers use. For instance, by identifying and compromising the software used to coordinate attacks, defenders can **neutralize** the adversary's ability to carry out large-scale operations. This tactic disrupts their operational capacity and forces them to rebuild or redesign their tools, buying defenders time to strengthen their own security posture.

Legal and Ethical Considerations in Offensive Cyber Tactics

The use of **offensive cyber tactics** raises a host of **legal** and **ethical concerns**. While offensive cyber operations can be an effective means of defending against attacks, they must be conducted within a framework that respects the **rule of law**, avoids **collateral damage**, and minimizes the risk of **escalation**.

1. LEGAL CONSIDERATIONS

Many countries have strict laws governing the use of offensive cyber tactics, particularly when it comes to **hack-back operations** or **preemptive strikes**. These activities may violate **cybercrime laws**, **data protection regulations**, and **international agreements**.

- **Unauthorized Access**:
In most jurisdictions, **unauthorized access** to a computer system is illegal, even if it is done in retaliation for an attack. Organizations must be aware of the legal frameworks that govern offensive cyber actions in their country and ensure that any preemptive or retaliatory strikes are conducted within the bounds of the law.
- **Attribution and Due Diligence**:
Offensive cyber operations require **accurate attribution** of

the attacker's identity and location. Engaging in offensive tactics without clear attribution risks targeting the wrong entities, leading to **legal liabilities** and potential harm to innocent parties.

- **Government Authorization**:
  In many cases, offensive cyber operations may need to be conducted with **government authorization**. Some governments, such as the United States, have specific policies that allow for **cyber counterattacks**, but these operations are typically restricted to military or intelligence agencies.

2. ETHICAL CONSIDERATIONS

Beyond the legal implications, there are also important **ethical questions** surrounding the use of offensive cyber tactics. Organizations must consider the potential consequences of their actions and ensure that their offensive operations are **proportionate**, **targeted**, and **justified**.

- **Collateral Damage**:
  Offensive cyber operations can inadvertently cause harm to third parties, particularly if the attacker's infrastructure is hosted on **compromised systems** or **botnets** that belong to innocent users. Ethical cyber operations must minimize the risk of **collateral damage** and avoid causing harm to civilians or non-combatants.
- **Proportionality**:
  Any offensive cyber operation must be **proportionate** to the threat posed by the adversary. Retaliating with overwhelming force or launching large-scale cyberattacks in response to a relatively minor intrusion could lead to **escalation** and create broader geopolitical or legal challenges.
- **Responsibility and Accountability**:
  Organizations engaging in offensive cyber operations must take responsibility for their actions and ensure that there is a

clear **chain of command** and **accountability**. This includes documenting the decision-making process, assessing the potential risks, and ensuring that the operation is conducted ethically and within the law.

CONCLUSION: OFFENSIVE CYBER CAPABILITIES IN MODERN DEFENSE STRATEGIES

Offensive cyber capabilities represent a powerful tool for defending against sophisticated cyber threats. By **disrupting adversary infrastructures**, engaging in **preemptive strikes**, and deploying **hack-back tactics** when necessary, organizations can take a proactive approach to defense. However, these tactics must be used judiciously, with a clear understanding of the **legal** and **ethical frameworks** that govern them.

As cyber threats continue to evolve, the ability to go on the offensive will become an increasingly important aspect of **cyber defense**. Offensive operations can help neutralize attackers before they can launch devastating attacks, disrupt their operations, and serve as a deterrent against future threats. However, organizations must carefully balance the benefits of offensive tactics with the risks of **escalation**, **collateral damage**, and potential **legal repercussions**.

CHAPTER 12: SECURING AI MODELS FROM ADVERSARIAL ATTACKS

INTRODUCTION

As **Artificial Intelligence (AI)** continues to transform industries and drive innovations in cybersecurity, healthcare, finance, and autonomous systems, it has also become a prime target for attackers. AI models, especially those that use **machine learning (ML)**, **deep learning (DL)**, and **neural networks**, are vulnerable to a range of sophisticated attacks known as **adversarial attacks**. These attacks exploit the underlying weaknesses in the algorithms, training data, and decision-making processes of AI models, leading to **misclassifications**, **malfunctioning systems**, or **biased outcomes**.

The security of AI systems is now a critical concern, as adversarial attacks on AI models can have serious consequences—ranging from **data breaches** and **financial losses** to **physical harm** in the case of autonomous vehicles or medical AI. Understanding the **vulnerabilities** of AI models, how **adversarial machine learning (AML) attacks** work, and developing **defense strategies** is essential for securing AI systems in a world where they are increasingly deployed in critical applications.

In this chapter, we will explore the vulnerabilities of AI models, how adversarial attacks work and continue to evolve, and the defense mechanisms that can be employed to protect AI systems. We will also discuss how **continuous monitoring** and **reinforcement learning** can be used to enhance the security and resilience of AI models.

Understanding the Vulnerabilities of AI Models

AI models, particularly those based on **machine learning** and **deep learning**, are highly dependent on data to learn and make decisions. This dependency on data introduces several inherent **vulnerabilities** that attackers can exploit. These vulnerabilities arise from the complexity of the models, the quality of the training data, and the limitations of current AI algorithms.

1. THE BLACK-BOX NATURE OF AI

One of the primary vulnerabilities of AI models is their **black-box nature**. Many AI systems, especially deep learning models, are highly complex, making it difficult to understand how they arrive at specific decisions. This lack of transparency makes it challenging to identify and fix vulnerabilities in the system.

- **Opacity in Decision-Making**:
  Deep learning models, for instance, are composed of multiple layers of neurons that process data in complex ways. The model's decision-making process is often opaque, making it difficult for even the model's designers to understand why a particular output was generated. This opacity can be exploited by attackers who can manipulate inputs to produce specific outputs without being detected.
- **Overfitting and Data Dependency**:
  AI models are often trained on large datasets that are assumed to be representative of the real world. However, if the training data is not diverse enough, or if it contains biases, the model can become **overfitted**—meaning it performs well on the training data but poorly on new, unseen data. Attackers can exploit this by crafting inputs that fall outside the distribution of the training data, leading the model to make incorrect predictions.

2. DEPENDENCY ON TRAINING DATA

AI models are highly dependent on the **quality and integrity of their training data**. If the training data is compromised, incomplete, or biased, the model will learn and make decisions based on flawed information.

- **Poisoned Training Data**:
  One of the most significant vulnerabilities in AI systems is the potential for **data poisoning** attacks. In these attacks, adversaries intentionally introduce **malicious data** into the training set to influence the model's learning process. This can lead the model to make incorrect predictions or classifications, with severe consequences in applications like fraud detection, medical diagnostics, or autonomous driving.

- **Bias in Data**:
  Even without malicious intent, biased training data can lead to flawed models. If the data used to train an AI model contains **inherent biases** (e.g., underrepresentation of certain demographic groups), the model will reproduce and even amplify these biases in its decision-making. Attackers can exploit these biases to manipulate the model's predictions in specific contexts.

3. INPUT SENSITIVITY

AI models, particularly those used for **image recognition, natural language processing,** and **speech recognition**, are highly sensitive to their inputs. This sensitivity can be exploited by attackers using **adversarial examples**—specially crafted inputs designed to trick the model into making incorrect predictions.

- **Adversarial Examples**:
  An **adversarial example** is an input that has been intentionally perturbed in a way that is imperceptible to humans but causes the AI model to make a significant error. For example, small, seemingly insignificant changes to the pixels of an image can cause a model to misclassify it entirely (e.g., classifying an image of a dog as a car). These examples highlight the vulnerability of AI models to subtle, targeted attacks.

ADVERSARIAL MACHINE LEARNING ATTACKS: HOW THEY WORK AND HOW THEY ARE EVOLVING

Adversarial machine learning (AML) is a rapidly growing field where attackers seek to exploit the weaknesses of AI models by manipulating inputs, training data, or the model itself to achieve malicious outcomes. As AI becomes more integrated into critical systems, AML attacks are becoming more sophisticated and varied.

1. TYPES OF ADVERSARIAL ATTACKS

There are several types of adversarial attacks that can be used to exploit AI models. These attacks can be broadly categorized based on the attacker's knowledge of the model (black-box vs. white-box attacks) and the type of manipulation they perform (input manipulation, poisoning, etc.).

- **White-Box Attacks**:
  In a **white-box attack**, the attacker has full knowledge of the AI model's architecture, parameters, and training data. This allows the attacker to craft highly targeted adversarial examples that are specifically designed to exploit the model's vulnerabilities. White-box attacks are particularly dangerous because they allow attackers to generate adversarial inputs that are almost guaranteed to succeed.
- **Black-Box Attacks**:
  In a **black-box attack**, the attacker does not have access to the model's internal workings and must rely on observing the model's outputs to craft adversarial examples. Black-box attacks are more challenging for attackers but still possible, especially through **query-based** methods where attackers repeatedly query the model with different inputs to infer its behavior.
- **Evasion Attacks**:
  In an **evasion attack**, the attacker modifies the input data in such a way that the AI model **misclassifies** it. For example, in image recognition systems, an attacker might subtly alter the pixels of an image to cause the model to misidentify it. These attacks are particularly effective against models used in **security systems**, such as facial recognition or biometric authentication.
- **Poisoning Attacks**:
  Data poisoning attacks involve the deliberate insertion of **malicious data** into the training set to influence the AI model's learning process. The goal is to train the model to

behave in a way that benefits the attacker, such as misclassifying certain types of inputs or making incorrect decisions under specific conditions.
- **Model Inversion Attacks**:
In a **model inversion attack**, the attacker uses the model's outputs to **reverse-engineer** sensitive information about the training data. This can be particularly dangerous in privacy-sensitive applications, where an attacker might be able to infer details about individual users from the model's predictions.

2. EVOLVING TECHNIQUES IN ADVERSARIAL MACHINE LEARNING

Adversarial machine learning is an **arms race** between attackers and defenders, with both sides constantly evolving their techniques. As defensive strategies improve, attackers are developing more sophisticated methods to bypass security measures.

- **Transferability of Adversarial Examples**:
One of the key discoveries in AML research is the concept of **transferability**—the idea that adversarial examples crafted for one model can often fool other models trained on similar data. This means that attackers can generate adversarial examples using one model (which they have access to) and successfully use them against a different, unseen model (such as a commercial AI system).
- **Adaptive Attacks**:
As defenders develop techniques to identify and mitigate adversarial examples, attackers have started using **adaptive attacks** that dynamically adjust the adversarial inputs based on the model's defenses. For example, an attacker might use **gradient-based optimization** to craft adversarial examples that evade detection by existing defenses.
- **Physical World Attacks**:
Adversarial attacks are not limited to the digital realm. **Physical world attacks** involve creating adversarial inputs that work in real-world settings. For example, attackers might

place stickers on a stop sign to trick an autonomous vehicle's computer vision system into misclassifying the sign. These attacks are particularly concerning for AI systems deployed in critical environments such as transportation, healthcare, or defense.

DEFENSE STRATEGIES AGAINST ADVERSARIAL ATTACKS

As adversarial machine learning attacks evolve, so too must the **defensive strategies** employed to protect AI models. Defenders must take a multi-layered approach to securing AI systems, incorporating both **technical solutions** and **best practices** for AI model development.

1. ADVERSARIAL TRAINING

Adversarial training is one of the most widely used defense techniques against adversarial attacks. It involves training the AI model not only on clean data but also on **adversarial examples**. By including adversarial examples in the training process, the model becomes more robust to perturbations and can better resist future attacks.

- **Augmenting the Training Dataset**:
  In adversarial training, the defender generates a set of adversarial examples using known attack methods and includes them in the training dataset. The model learns to recognize and correctly classify these examples, improving its overall robustness.
- **Iterative Adversarial Training**:
  One of the challenges of adversarial training is that it must be **iterative** to keep up with evolving attacks. New adversarial examples are constantly being developed, so the training process must be regularly updated with fresh examples to maintain effectiveness.

2. DEFENSIVE DISTILLATION

Defensive distillation is a technique that aims to make AI models more resistant to adversarial attacks by **smoothing out** the decision boundaries of the model. This is done by training the model on the **soft outputs** (probabilities) of a more complex model, rather than directly on the hard labels of the training data.

- **Smoothing Decision Boundaries**:
  By using soft outputs (i.e., probability distributions) instead of hard labels, defensive distillation reduces the model's sensitivity to small perturbations in the input. This makes it harder for adversarial examples to push the model's predictions over the decision boundary.
- **Reducing Overfitting**:
  Defensive distillation can also help reduce **overfitting**, as it encourages the model to generalize better to unseen examples. This can mitigate the effectiveness of adversarial attacks that rely on exploiting overfitting or bias in the training data.

3. ROBUST OPTIMIZATION TECHNIQUES

Robust optimization techniques focus on improving the model's ability to handle **noisy** or **perturbed data**. These techniques include using **regularization** methods, such as **L2 regularization**, that penalize overly complex models and reduce the risk of adversarial exploitation.

- **Gradient Masking**:
  Gradient masking is a technique used to make it harder for attackers to craft adversarial examples by obscuring the gradient information that attackers rely on to optimize their inputs. By reducing the sensitivity of the model's predictions to small changes in the input, gradient masking can make it more difficult for adversarial examples to succeed.

- **Randomization**:
  Another effective defense strategy is **randomization**—introducing random noise or transformations into the input data to disrupt the attacker's ability to create precise adversarial examples. For instance, randomizing the order of pixels in an image or adding slight noise to the input can prevent adversarial perturbations from having the desired effect.

4. AI MODEL AUDITING AND EXPLAINABILITY

AI models are often vulnerable to adversarial attacks due to their **lack of transparency**. Enhancing the **explainability** of AI models—understanding how and why they make certain predictions—can help defenders identify and address vulnerabilities.

- **Model Auditing**:
  Regular **audits** of AI models can help identify potential weaknesses before attackers can exploit them. Auditing involves testing the model against a variety of adversarial examples and conducting **stress tests** to determine how the model responds to unexpected inputs.
- **Explainability Tools**:
  Tools that provide insights into the **decision-making process** of AI models (such as **SHAP** or **LIME**) can help defenders understand how the model is interpreting inputs. This understanding is critical for identifying potential attack vectors and improving the model's robustness.

Continuous Monitoring and Reinforcement Learning for AI Security

Defending AI models from adversarial attacks is not a one-time effort—it requires **continuous monitoring** and the use of adaptive techniques, such as **reinforcement learning**, to enhance security over time. By continuously monitoring the performance and behavior of AI models, defenders can detect **anomalies** and **potential attacks** before they escalate.

1. CONTINUOUS MONITORING OF AI MODELS

Monitoring AI models in real-time is essential for detecting potential adversarial attacks as they occur. By continuously evaluating the model's outputs and performance, defenders can identify when the model is being targeted by adversarial inputs.

- **Anomaly Detection Systems:**
  Anomaly detection systems can be used to monitor the AI model's behavior and flag any deviations from expected patterns. For example, if the model starts making unusually high numbers of misclassifications or if its performance suddenly degrades, this may indicate an ongoing adversarial attack.
- **Model Health Monitoring:**
  Monitoring the **health** of AI models includes tracking **accuracy, confidence levels**, and other key metrics. If the model's accuracy drops unexpectedly or if its predictions become erratic, defenders can investigate the issue and determine whether an adversarial attack is to blame.

2. REINFORCEMENT LEARNING FOR ADAPTIVE SECURITY

Reinforcement learning (RL) is a powerful tool for improving the security of AI models over time. RL involves training an AI model to **learn from its environment** and **adapt its behavior** based on feedback. In the context of security, reinforcement learning can be used to continuously improve the model's ability to detect and defend against adversarial attacks.

- **Self-Improving Defenses:**
  Reinforcement learning enables AI models to develop **self-improving defenses** by learning from past attacks and

adjusting their strategies accordingly. For example, if an attacker successfully deploys an adversarial example, the model can learn from the attack and adjust its parameters to prevent similar attacks in the future.
- **Dynamic Security Policies**:
RL can also be used to develop **dynamic security policies** that evolve over time based on the changing threat landscape. These policies can include adaptive techniques for detecting adversarial examples, adjusting model hyperparameters, or deploying new defense strategies as attacks evolve.

Conclusion: Securing AI in an Adversarial World

As AI becomes increasingly integrated into critical systems, securing AI models from **adversarial attacks** is more important than ever. Understanding the **vulnerabilities** of AI models and the **techniques used by attackers** is the first step in building a robust defense.

By employing a combination of **adversarial training, defensive distillation, robust optimization,** and **continuous monitoring,** defenders can significantly improve the resilience of AI models against adversarial attacks. Moreover, using **reinforcement learning** and **adaptive security policies** allows AI models to evolve and learn from attacks, enhancing their long-term security.

In a world where AI is both a target and a tool in cyber defense, maintaining the security of AI systems is critical for ensuring their safe and reliable operation. By staying ahead of adversaries and continually improving defensive techniques, organizations can secure their AI models and protect the systems and data they depend on.

CHAPTER 13: AI GOVERNANCE AND ETHICAL CONSIDERATIONS IN CYBER DEFENSE

Introduction

As **Artificial Intelligence (AI)** becomes an indispensable part of modern cybersecurity operations, it is essential to address the **ethical considerations** and **governance frameworks** that must accompany its use. AI-driven systems have the power to autonomously detect threats, make decisions, and take actions in real-time to defend against cyberattacks. While this brings significant benefits in terms of speed, efficiency, and accuracy, it also introduces **risks** related to **transparency, bias, accountability**, and the **potential for misuse**.

AI models, particularly those involved in critical security operations, must adhere to **ethical principles** that prioritize fairness, transparency, and the minimization of harm. Inadequate governance and oversight of AI systems can lead to unintended consequences, such as biased decision-making, disproportionate targeting of certain groups, and errors in classification that could lead to significant security breaches. Additionally, the **autonomy** of AI systems in high-stakes scenarios, such as national defense or critical infrastructure protection, raises concerns about **accountability** and the role of **human oversight**.

In this chapter, we will discuss the **importance of ethical AI** in the context of cybersecurity, how to establish effective **AI governance frameworks** to mitigate risks, the importance of **preventing bias** and ensuring **transparency** in AI-driven defense systems, and the balance between **AI autonomy** and **human oversight** in critical systems. By addressing these issues, organizations can develop robust AI-driven defenses that are not only effective but also responsible and accountable.

The Importance of Ethical AI in Cybersecurity

In the world of cybersecurity, the rapid integration of AI into defense systems brings new ethical challenges. **Ethical AI** is crucial because these systems often operate with little human intervention, making decisions that can have far-reaching consequences. Ethical AI must ensure that the decisions made by AI-driven systems are **fair, just,** and **aligned with societal values**.

1. Trust in AI-Driven Defense Systems

One of the most critical aspects of ethical AI in cybersecurity is ensuring **trust** in the decisions made by AI systems. Trust is built on the foundation of **accuracy, transparency,** and **fairness** in decision-making. In cybersecurity, AI systems may be tasked with detecting threats, allocating resources, or even engaging in autonomous response actions against attackers. If these systems are not governed by clear ethical principles, they risk undermining the very security they are designed to protect.

- **Decision-Making Accountability:**
  AI systems must be designed to provide **accountability** for their decisions, especially in scenarios where these decisions involve automated responses to perceived threats. Without accountability, it is difficult to determine whether an AI system's decision was **fair, proportional,** or **necessary**. This is especially important in systems that autonomously trigger responses, such as blocking network traffic, shutting down critical systems, or retaliating against cyberattacks.
- **Preventing Harm and Minimizing Collateral Damage:**
  Ethical AI in cybersecurity must prioritize minimizing harm, particularly when it comes to **collateral damage**. For instance, in the case of an AI-driven intrusion detection system, an ethical AI model would ensure that defensive actions do not inadvertently harm legitimate users or cause unnecessary

disruption to business operations. This balance between defense and harm prevention is critical in ensuring the system's overall ethical integrity.

2. FAIRNESS AND INCLUSIVITY IN CYBER DEFENSE

AI systems used in cybersecurity must also be designed to be **fair** and **inclusive** in their decision-making processes. This means ensuring that AI models do not disproportionately target certain individuals or groups based on biased data or flawed algorithms.

- **Avoiding Discriminatory Practices**:
  AI systems in cybersecurity must avoid making decisions that disproportionately impact specific demographics, organizations, or geographical regions. For instance, if a security system is trained on biased data that overrepresents certain types of threats, it may unfairly target or scrutinize certain groups. This could lead to **discriminatory practices** where certain users are unfairly blocked or penalized due to the biases embedded in the AI system.
- **Promoting Equal Treatment**:
  Ethical AI in cybersecurity should promote **equal treatment** by ensuring that all users are protected from cyber threats regardless of their identity, status, or geographic location. In cases where AI systems are deployed across global networks, it is essential to design models that are sensitive to **cultural** and **contextual differences** to avoid creating unintended disadvantages for specific user groups.

By prioritizing **ethical considerations** in AI-driven cybersecurity systems, organizations can ensure that their defensive tools operate in a manner that upholds fairness, transparency, and the protection of individual rights.

ESTABLISHING AI GOVERNANCE FRAMEWORKS TO MITIGATE RISKS

To effectively manage the **risks** associated with AI in cybersecurity, it is essential to establish **AI governance frameworks** that provide clear guidelines for the **development, deployment,** and **monitoring** of AI systems. Governance frameworks ensure that AI technologies are used responsibly and that there are mechanisms in place to address **bias, accountability,** and **risk management.**

1. THE ROLE OF GOVERNANCE IN AI

AI governance refers to the set of **policies, processes,** and **practices** that ensure AI systems are developed and used in a manner consistent with ethical principles and organizational goals. In cybersecurity, AI governance frameworks are essential for mitigating risks related to the **misuse** of AI, ensuring **compliance** with legal regulations, and maintaining **public trust** in AI-driven defense mechanisms.

- Governance Structures:
  Organizations should establish clear **governance structures** that define who is responsible for overseeing AI systems, including **ethics boards, compliance officers,** and **technical experts**. These structures should ensure that AI models are regularly evaluated for their effectiveness, security, and ethical alignment.
- AI Risk Assessment:
  Governance frameworks should include **AI risk assessment** procedures that evaluate the potential risks associated with deploying AI systems in cybersecurity environments. This assessment should consider the potential for **adversarial attacks** on AI models, the risk of **bias** in decision-making, and the potential for **unintended consequences** such as the over-blocking of legitimate users.

2. BEST PRACTICES FOR AI GOVERNANCE

Several best practices can be implemented as part of an AI governance framework to ensure the **responsible use of AI** in cybersecurity:

- **Ethical AI Guidelines**:
  Establishing **ethical AI guidelines** provides a foundation for the development and deployment of AI systems. These guidelines should outline principles such as **transparency, fairness, accountability,** and **non-discrimination**. By adhering to these principles, organizations can ensure that AI systems operate within the boundaries of ethical conduct.
- **Continuous Evaluation and Auditing**:
  AI governance frameworks must include processes for the **continuous evaluation** and **auditing** of AI systems. This includes regularly testing AI models for potential biases, assessing their performance in real-world scenarios, and conducting **security audits** to identify vulnerabilities. Regular audits help to ensure that AI systems remain compliant with governance standards and operate effectively over time.
- **Risk Mitigation Strategies**:
  AI governance frameworks should incorporate **risk mitigation strategies** that address the potential for AI systems to cause harm. This includes designing AI models with **fail-safes** and **contingency plans** in place to minimize the impact of incorrect decisions or unexpected outcomes. For example, if an AI system mistakenly classifies a legitimate user as a threat, there should be mechanisms to quickly **correct** the decision and prevent harm.

By establishing **robust AI governance frameworks**, organizations can manage the risks associated with AI-driven cybersecurity systems and ensure that these systems operate ethically and effectively.

Preventing Bias and Ensuring Transparency in AI-Driven Defense Systems

One of the most significant challenges in deploying AI in cybersecurity is the risk of **bias** in AI models. Biased AI systems can lead to **discriminatory outcomes**, where certain groups or individuals are unfairly targeted or misclassified based on flawed data or algorithms. Additionally, the **lack of transparency** in many AI models—especially **black-box models**—makes it difficult to identify and address these biases.

1. THE CHALLENGE OF BIAS IN AI SYSTEMS

Bias in AI systems can arise from several sources, including the **data used to train the models**, the **algorithms themselves**, and the **human decision-makers** involved in developing and deploying AI systems. In the context of cybersecurity, bias can manifest in several ways:

- **Data Bias:**
  AI models are often trained on large datasets, which may contain **inherent biases**. For example, if the training data disproportionately represents certain types of threats or behaviors, the AI model may become biased toward detecting those threats while missing others. This can lead to the **over-policing** of certain users or activities while **under-protecting** others.
- **Algorithmic Bias:**
  Even if the training data is unbiased, the algorithms used to process the data can introduce biases. Some algorithms may place more weight on certain features than others, leading to biased outcomes. For instance, an AI model designed to detect insider threats might overemphasize certain behaviors (such as accessing sensitive files) without accounting for legitimate use cases, leading to false positives.

2. ENSURING TRANSPARENCY AND EXPLAINABILITY IN AI MODELS

To address the issue of bias, it is crucial to ensure **transparency** and **explainability** in AI-driven defense systems. **Explainability** refers to the ability to understand and interpret how an AI model makes decisions, while **transparency** involves making the inner workings of AI systems visible and understandable to stakeholders.

- **Explainable AI (XAI):**
  Explainable AI aims to create models that are interpretable and understandable by humans. In cybersecurity, this means developing AI models that can explain **why** they flagged certain behaviors as suspicious or took specific actions to mitigate threats. This level of transparency is essential for identifying potential biases and ensuring that the model's decisions can be **justified**.
- **Auditing AI Models for Bias:**
  Regular audits of AI models are essential to identify and address biases in the system. Auditing involves testing the AI model on a variety of inputs to determine whether it is disproportionately targeting certain groups or making biased decisions. This process helps to **ensure fairness** and **prevent discrimination** in AI-driven cybersecurity systems.
- **Data Diversity:**
  One of the most effective ways to prevent bias in AI models is to ensure that the training data is **diverse** and **representative** of the real-world environments in which the AI system will operate. This means including a wide range of threat types, user behaviors, and environmental factors in the training data to ensure that the AI model can make balanced and fair decisions.

By promoting **transparency, explainability,** and **fairness,** organizations can develop AI-driven defense systems that are free from bias and operate in a manner that is **ethical** and **accountable**.

Balancing AI Autonomy with Human Oversight in Critical Systems

As AI systems become more **autonomous** and are increasingly relied upon in **critical cybersecurity** operations, it is important to balance AI autonomy with **human oversight**. AI-driven systems have the potential to make decisions faster and more accurately than humans, but they are not infallible. Human oversight is essential to ensure that AI systems are making **correct, ethical**, and **proportionate** decisions, especially in high-stakes scenarios.

1. THE ROLE OF HUMAN OVERSIGHT IN AI-DRIVEN CYBERSECURITY

Human oversight is critical in ensuring that AI-driven cybersecurity systems are held accountable and that their actions are aligned with ethical and legal standards. Even the most advanced AI systems may make errors or misinterpret data, leading to incorrect decisions that could have severe consequences.

- **Human-in-the-Loop (HITL) Systems**:
  One of the ways to balance AI autonomy with human oversight is by implementing **human-in-the-loop** systems. In these systems, AI models provide recommendations or take preliminary actions, but final decisions are made or approved by **human operators**. For example, in a system that automatically detects and responds to potential cyberattacks, a human operator might review the AI's decisions before allowing it to block network traffic or isolate a compromised system.
- **Human-on-the-Loop (HOTL) Systems**:
  Another approach is **human-on-the-loop** systems, where AI operates autonomously, but human operators maintain **real-time oversight** and can intervene if necessary. In this model, humans do not need to approve every decision, but they have the authority to **override** the AI system if it is making an incorrect or harmful decision.

2. THE RISKS OF UNCHECKED AI AUTONOMY

While autonomous AI systems offer significant advantages in terms of speed and efficiency, there are risks associated with allowing AI systems to operate **without sufficient oversight**. These risks include:

- **Overreliance on AI**:
  One of the dangers of fully autonomous AI systems is that human operators may become **over-reliant** on the AI and fail to question its decisions. This can lead to a lack of **critical thinking** and an inability to recognize when the AI is making mistakes or acting on flawed data.
- **Ethical and Legal Accountability**:
  Fully autonomous AI systems also raise questions about **accountability**. If an AI system makes a decision that leads to harm, it may be unclear who is responsible—the developers, the operators, or the organization as a whole. Balancing autonomy with human oversight ensures that there is always a **human decision-maker** who is ultimately responsible for the AI's actions.

3. COMBINING AI AUTONOMY WITH ETHICAL GUARDRAILS

To ensure that AI systems operate ethically and responsibly, organizations should combine AI autonomy with **ethical guardrails**—guidelines and frameworks that define the boundaries within which the AI system can operate.

- **Predefined Ethical Boundaries**:
  AI systems should be programmed with **predefined ethical boundaries** that restrict their actions in certain situations. For example, an AI system might be prohibited from taking actions that could result in harm to innocent parties or from deploying offensive cyber operations without human approval.
- **Real-Time Monitoring and Auditing**:
  Even in fully autonomous systems, **real-time monitoring** and

auditing are essential to ensure that AI models are operating within the defined ethical boundaries. This allows human operators to detect and correct any deviations from acceptable behavior.

By maintaining a balance between **AI autonomy** and **human oversight**, organizations can ensure that AI-driven cybersecurity systems operate efficiently while remaining **accountable, ethical,** and **aligned with organizational values.**

Conclusion: The Path Forward for Ethical AI in Cyber Defense

As AI continues to revolutionize the field of cybersecurity, it is imperative that organizations establish **ethical frameworks** and **governance structures** to ensure that AI-driven defense systems are deployed responsibly. By prioritizing **ethical considerations**, including **fairness, transparency,** and **accountability**, organizations can build AI systems that not only protect against cyber threats but also uphold the values of **trust** and **justice**.

Establishing **AI governance frameworks** ensures that risks are properly managed, biases are minimized, and AI systems remain secure and reliable. Preventing **bias** and ensuring **transparency** are critical to building AI models that treat all users equitably and make decisions based on a clear and justifiable rationale.

Finally, balancing **AI autonomy** with **human oversight** in critical systems ensures that AI-driven decisions are subject to human review and correction, particularly in high-stakes scenarios where errors could have severe consequences. This balance will be key as AI continues to advance, allowing us to harness its full potential while safeguarding against unintended harm.

CHAPTER 14: AI ROBUSTNESS AND RESILIENCE IN A CYBERWARFARE CONTEXT

INTRODUCTION

As **Artificial Intelligence (AI)** becomes more deeply integrated into **cyber defense** and **military operations**, ensuring the **robustness** and **resilience** of AI models in the face of adversarial attacks has become a top priority. In a **cyberwarfare context**, where nation-states, well-funded cybercriminal organizations, and highly skilled attackers target AI-driven systems, the ability to withstand and recover from attacks is critical for maintaining operational continuity and security.

AI systems, particularly those employed in **cyber defense**, must be designed not only to **resist attacks** but also to **adapt and recover** from failures or adversarial attempts to exploit vulnerabilities. This requires the development of **robust models** that can handle a variety of **adversarial threats**—from direct attacks on the model itself to **AI-powered attacks** launched by sophisticated adversaries. Additionally, building **resilient AI systems** involves incorporating **redundancy** and **diversity** to ensure that even if one component of the AI infrastructure fails, the system as a whole can continue functioning.

This chapter will explore how to build AI models that are robust enough to withstand attacks, how to enhance resilience through redundancy and diversity, how to **test AI models** against adversarial threats using simulation environments, and how AI can play a critical role in detecting and countering AI-driven cyberattacks.

BUILDING ROBUST AI MODELS THAT CAN WITHSTAND ATTACKS

Robustness in AI refers to the model's ability to perform reliably even in the presence of **adversarial perturbations**, **noise**, or unexpected inputs. In a cyberwarfare context, AI systems will likely be exposed to **adversarial machine learning (AML)** attacks that seek to manipulate the model's inputs or exploit its decision-making process. Therefore, building robust AI models is essential for ensuring that these systems can maintain **accuracy, stability**, and **security** under attack.

1. DEFENDING AGAINST ADVERSARIAL EXAMPLES

Adversarial examples are specially crafted inputs designed to deceive AI models into making incorrect predictions. These subtle changes to inputs—often imperceptible to humans—can cause AI systems to misclassify images, misinterpret signals, or make faulty decisions. Defending against these attacks requires a combination of **model improvements, regularization techniques**, and **defensive training**.

- **Adversarial Training**:
  One of the most effective methods for increasing the robustness of AI models is **adversarial training**. In this process, the AI model is trained not only on clean data but also on adversarially perturbed data. By incorporating these **adversarial examples** into the training set, the model learns to recognize and correctly classify such inputs, making it less vulnerable to attacks. Adversarial training can be *iterative*, with the model continuously exposed to new adversarial strategies over time.
- **Regularization and Robust Optimization**:
  Regularization techniques like **L2 regularization** can help prevent models from becoming overly sensitive to small changes in input data. These techniques penalize the model's complexity, making it more resilient to perturbations. Additionally, **robust optimization** methods focus on training AI models to be less sensitive to outliers and adversarial noise, further enhancing their robustness.
- **Defensive Distillation**:
  Defensive distillation is another technique used to make AI

models more robust to adversarial examples. By training the model on the **soft outputs** (probability distributions) of a more complex model, rather than hard labels, the model's decision boundaries are **smoothed out**, making it harder for attackers to find weaknesses that can be exploited.

2. ROBUSTNESS IN AI MODEL ARCHITECTURES

Designing **robust architectures** is another crucial step in building AI systems that can withstand attacks. This involves selecting architectures that are naturally resistant to certain types of adversarial attacks and implementing mechanisms that ensure **model integrity** under duress.

- **Ensemble Models**:
  One approach to enhancing robustness is to use **ensemble models**, where multiple AI models are combined to make predictions. Since different models are likely to have different vulnerabilities, combining their outputs can mitigate the risk of adversarial manipulation. **Model averaging** or **majority voting** techniques can be employed to ensure that the final decision reflects the consensus of multiple models, reducing the effectiveness of adversarial examples.
- **Redundant Feature Extraction**:
  AI models can be made more robust by using **redundant feature extraction**, where the model learns from multiple redundant inputs or features. This reduces the likelihood that a small perturbation to a single feature will lead to a large shift in the model's output. By making predictions based on a diverse set of features, AI models can better resist adversarial attacks that attempt to exploit weaknesses in individual input features.

Building robust AI models involves a combination of **model architecture design**, **defensive training**, and **regularization techniques** that enhance the model's ability to resist attacks and maintain accuracy under adversarial conditions.

Enhancing Resilience Through Redundancy and Diversity in AI Systems

In addition to robustness, **resilience** is a key consideration when deploying AI systems in a **cyberwarfare context**. Resilience refers to the AI system's ability to **recover** from disruptions, maintain **continuity of operations**, and adapt to changing conditions. In a cyberattack scenario, AI-driven defense systems may come under **direct attack**, making it essential that these systems incorporate **redundancy** and **diversity** to ensure their continued operation.

1. REDUNDANCY IN AI SYSTEMS

Redundancy involves having **backup systems, spare capacity**, or **duplicated components** that can take over when the primary system is compromised or fails. In the context of AI, redundancy can be implemented at multiple levels, from **data storage** to **model architectures**.

- **Model Redundancy**:
  One approach to increasing resilience is to use **multiple AI models** that operate in parallel. If one model is compromised or fails due to an adversarial attack, another model can take over the decision-making process. This ensures that the system remains operational, even if part of the AI infrastructure is affected. These models can be designed to function independently, each with its own training data, architecture, and defenses, ensuring that an attack on one model does not compromise the entire system.
- **Data Redundancy**:
  Data redundancy involves storing critical data in multiple locations, ensuring that the AI system can continue to function even if part of the data infrastructure is compromised. For example, sensitive training data or model parameters could be stored in distributed databases or

backed up across multiple cloud environments. This reduces the risk of **data tampering** or **corruption** during a cyberattack.

2. DIVERSITY IN AI SYSTEMS

Diversity in AI systems involves using a variety of models, architectures, and algorithms to increase the system's overall resilience. By relying on diverse approaches, AI systems become less vulnerable to attacks that target specific weaknesses in a particular model or algorithm.

- **Algorithmic Diversity**:
  In many AI-driven cybersecurity systems, a single algorithm may be responsible for detecting threats, making decisions, or responding to attacks. However, attackers can target the specific weaknesses of that algorithm. **Algorithmic diversity** mitigates this risk by using different algorithms to perform similar tasks, making it harder for attackers to exploit any single vulnerability. For example, one algorithm might use **supervised learning** for threat detection, while another employs **unsupervised learning** to detect anomalies. By combining these approaches, the system becomes more resilient.
- **Diversity in Training Data**:
  Another aspect of diversity involves ensuring that AI models are trained on a wide range of **diverse data**. Diverse training data helps models generalize better, reducing the risk of overfitting to specific attack patterns. It also makes the system more adaptable to new types of adversarial examples. In a cyberwarfare context, this means training AI models on data from **multiple sources** (e.g., various threat vectors, attack patterns, and geographical regions) to ensure that they are prepared to handle a wide range of threats.

By incorporating **redundancy** and **diversity** into AI systems, organizations can significantly enhance the resilience of their AI-driven defense infrastructure, ensuring that these systems remain functional and effective even in the face of sophisticated cyberattacks.

TESTING AI MODELS AGAINST ADVERSARIAL THREATS: SIMULATION AND TRAINING ENVIRONMENTS

To build robust and resilient AI systems, it is essential to **test** these models against **adversarial threats** using **simulation** and **training environments**. These environments allow developers and cybersecurity teams to assess the performance of AI models in realistic, high-stakes scenarios and identify potential weaknesses before they can be exploited by real-world attackers.

1. SIMULATING CYBERWARFARE SCENARIOS

Simulating **cyberwarfare scenarios** provides an opportunity to test AI models against a wide range of **threats**, including both **traditional attacks** (such as malware and ransomware) and **adversarial machine learning attacks**. By subjecting AI models to simulated attacks, defenders can observe how the models respond under stress and identify areas where improvements are needed.

- **Realistic Threat Modeling**:
  In a simulation environment, AI models can be exposed to **realistic threat scenarios** that mimic the tactics, techniques, and procedures (TTPs) used by real-world adversaries. This includes simulating **zero-day exploits, social engineering attacks**, and **AI-powered malware**. These scenarios allow defenders to test how well the AI model can detect and respond to **novel threats** and whether it can adapt to changing attack patterns in real-time.
- **Red Teaming**:
  Red teaming is a valuable technique for testing the resilience of AI models. In a red team exercise, a group of ethical hackers (the red team) attempts to exploit vulnerabilities in

the AI system, simulating the actions of real-world attackers. By engaging in red teaming exercises, organizations can identify weaknesses in their AI systems and refine their defenses accordingly. Red teaming also helps developers anticipate new types of adversarial attacks and improve the model's ability to resist them.

2. ADVERSARIAL TRAINING ENVIRONMENTS

In addition to simulating attacks, **adversarial training environments** provide a controlled setting where AI models can be trained and tested on **adversarial examples**. These environments allow defenders to continuously improve the robustness of AI models by exposing them to a variety of **attack strategies**.

- **Iterative Adversarial Training**:
  In adversarial training environments, AI models are iteratively exposed to new adversarial examples generated by **attack simulations**. Each iteration improves the model's ability to detect and counter adversarial attacks. Over time, the model becomes more robust to increasingly sophisticated adversarial strategies.
- **Scenario-Based Training**:
  Adversarial training environments also support **scenario-based training**, where AI models are tested against specific types of attacks (e.g., evasion attacks, poisoning attacks, or model inversion attacks). This targeted approach allows defenders to fine-tune the model's defenses for particular threat vectors and ensures that the system is well-prepared to handle the types of attacks most likely to be encountered in a cyberwarfare context.

By using **simulation** and **adversarial training environments**, organizations can test their AI models in realistic scenarios and continuously improve their defenses against adversarial threats.

The Role of AI in Detecting and Countering AI-Based Attacks

As **AI-based attacks** become more prevalent, AI itself is emerging as a critical tool for detecting and countering these sophisticated threats. Attackers are increasingly using AI to automate attacks, craft sophisticated phishing attempts, and generate **adversarial examples**. In this context, AI-driven defense systems must be capable of **identifying** and **neutralizing** AI-powered threats in real-time.

1. AI-Driven Threat Detection

AI can play a critical role in **threat detection**, particularly in identifying attacks that would be difficult for traditional cybersecurity tools to detect. AI models can analyze vast amounts of **network traffic, user behavior**, and **system logs** to identify subtle patterns that indicate the presence of an adversarial attack.

- **Anomaly Detection**:
  One of the primary ways AI is used in threat detection is through **anomaly detection**. By training AI models on normal patterns of network activity, defenders can detect deviations that may indicate a cyberattack. This is especially effective for identifying **zero-day attacks**, which often involve novel behaviors that do not match known signatures. AI models can detect these anomalies in real-time and trigger alerts or initiate automated responses.
- **Behavioral Analysis**:
  AI-driven systems can also analyze the behavior of **users** and **devices** to identify suspicious activities. For example, an AI system might detect that a user is accessing sensitive files at an unusual time or from an unfamiliar location, flagging this behavior as potentially malicious. By continuously monitoring user behavior, AI systems can detect the early signs of an attack and respond before significant damage is done.

2. COUNTERING AI-BASED ATTACKS

In addition to detecting AI-based attacks, AI systems are increasingly being used to **counter** these threats. This involves using AI to **automate defense strategies**, respond to **adversarial actions**, and even launch **countermeasures** against attackers.

- **Automated Response Systems:**
  AI can automate many aspects of **cyber defense**, from isolating compromised systems to blocking malicious traffic. When an AI system detects an attack, it can take immediate action to neutralize the threat, such as rerouting network traffic, deploying **honeypots**, or initiating a **rollback** of compromised systems. These **automated response systems** help reduce the time between detection and response, minimizing the impact of the attack.
- **Adaptive Defense Mechanisms:**
  AI can also be used to develop **adaptive defense mechanisms** that adjust in real-time based on the nature of the attack. For example, if an AI system detects that an adversary is using an AI-powered tool to launch a distributed denial-of-service (DDoS) attack, the system can adapt by dynamically increasing network capacity or redirecting traffic to minimize disruption.
- **AI vs. AI Warfare:**
  As attackers increasingly use AI to craft sophisticated attacks, defenders must also use AI to **counter AI-based threats**. This involves creating AI systems that can engage in **AI vs. AI warfare**, where defensive AI models anticipate and respond to attacks launched by malicious AI. This type of engagement requires AI systems that are capable of learning and adapting to adversarial actions in real-time, using techniques such as **reinforcement learning** to improve their defenses over time.

AI's role in **detecting** and **countering AI-based attacks** is essential for maintaining **cyber resilience** in a rapidly evolving threat landscape. By leveraging AI's ability to **analyze data**, **detect anomalies**, and

automate responses, organizations can stay ahead of attackers and defend their systems more effectively.

Conclusion: Building AI Robustness and Resilience in Cyberwarfare

In the context of **cyberwarfare**, building AI systems that are both **robust** and **resilient** is critical for maintaining **security, continuity of operations**, and **defense capabilities**. AI models must be designed to withstand **adversarial attacks**, recover from disruptions, and adapt to the ever-changing tactics of cyber adversaries.

By employing techniques such as **adversarial training, robust optimization**, and **defensive distillation**, organizations can build AI models that are better equipped to handle **adversarial examples** and **sophisticated threats**. Meanwhile, incorporating **redundancy** and **diversity** into AI systems ensures that these models can continue to operate even when parts of the infrastructure are compromised.

Testing AI models in **simulation environments** and subjecting them to **adversarial training** further strengthens their defenses, allowing organizations to identify vulnerabilities and improve their resilience. Additionally, AI-driven systems play a critical role in detecting and countering **AI-based attacks**, ensuring that defenders stay ahead of increasingly sophisticated adversaries.

As the use of AI in **cyberwarfare** continues to grow, building **robust** and **resilient** AI systems will be essential for protecting critical infrastructure, defending against nation-state actors, and maintaining **cybersecurity** in an increasingly hostile digital landscape.

CHAPTER 15: CYBERSECURITY AUTOMATION AND AI-DRIVEN OPTIMIZATION

Introduction

In today's fast-paced and ever-evolving cyber threat landscape, the need for **speed** and **efficiency** in defending against attacks is more critical than ever. Traditional manual approaches to cybersecurity are increasingly inadequate against the growing sophistication and volume of threats. **Artificial Intelligence (AI)** has emerged as a game-changing force, enabling organizations to automate key aspects of their cyber defense operations, streamline **incident response**, and adopt **proactive defense** strategies that detect and mitigate threats before they can cause damage.

By harnessing the power of **predictive analytics**, **Software Defined Networking (SDN)**, and **AI-driven automation**, cybersecurity teams can respond to threats in real-time, drastically reducing the time attackers have to exploit vulnerabilities. Additionally, by applying **guerrilla warfare-style tactics** such as **attrition warfare**—where defenders continuously wear down attackers through sustained defensive actions—organizations can keep attackers on the defensive, making it difficult for them to succeed.

In this chapter, we will explore how **AI** enables cybersecurity automation, the role of **predictive analytics** in proactive defense, how **SDN** facilitates automated incident response, and how to overwhelm attackers using **guerrilla-style attrition warfare**. By combining these approaches, organizations can significantly enhance their cyber defenses and stay ahead of adversaries in an increasingly hostile digital environment.

The Need for Speed: How AI Can Automate Defense Actions

In cybersecurity, the ability to **respond quickly** to threats is crucial for minimizing the potential damage caused by attacks. Manual processes, while thorough, are often too slow to keep up with modern threats such as **automated malware**, **ransomware**, and **advanced persistent threats (APTs)**, which can spread across networks in seconds. **AI-driven automation** offers a solution by enabling real-time detection and response to cyberattacks, reducing the **mean time to detect (MTTD)** and **mean time to respond (MTTR)**.

1. REAL-TIME THREAT DETECTION AND RESPONSE

AI excels at **real-time threat detection** by continuously monitoring network traffic, user behavior, and system logs for signs of suspicious activity. Traditional signature-based detection methods are reactive and often miss novel or zero-day threats. AI, on the other hand, uses **machine learning** and **anomaly detection** techniques to identify patterns and behaviors that deviate from the norm, allowing it to detect even previously unknown threats.

- **Behavioral Analysis**:
  AI-driven cybersecurity systems can analyze **user behavior** to identify abnormal activities such as unusual login times, unexpected file access, or abnormal network traffic. These anomalies may indicate a potential breach or insider threat. Once detected, AI systems can automatically initiate **remediation actions**, such as blocking suspicious users, locking compromised accounts, or isolating infected systems.
- **Automated Defense Actions**:
  Once a threat is detected, AI can automatically trigger **defense actions** based on pre-configured security policies. For instance, if an AI system detects a **ransomware attack**, it can immediately shut down affected systems, quarantine malicious files, and block traffic to command-and-control (C2) servers. This level of automation ensures that response

times are reduced to milliseconds, preventing attackers from causing widespread damage.

2. AI-POWERED DECISION-MAKING

AI can assist cybersecurity teams in making **quick decisions** by analyzing vast amounts of data and providing actionable insights in real-time. This allows defenders to focus on more complex and strategic tasks while AI handles routine detection, analysis, and response.

- **Risk-Based Decision Making**:
  AI can prioritize threats based on their **severity** and **potential impact**, helping cybersecurity teams focus on the most critical incidents. For example, an AI system might identify that an attempted SQL injection attack is low risk but that a data exfiltration attempt involving sensitive customer information requires immediate action. By automating this prioritization process, organizations can ensure that their resources are focused where they are needed most.
- **AI-Driven Automation Playbooks**:
  Many organizations are implementing **AI-driven automation playbooks**, which are pre-defined workflows that dictate how to respond to specific types of threats. These playbooks allow AI to automatically execute a series of actions—such as isolating compromised systems, notifying the security team, and logging evidence—whenever a predefined set of conditions is met.

By leveraging AI to **automate defense actions** and **speed up decision-making**, organizations can reduce their response times, contain threats more effectively, and minimize the potential damage caused by cyberattacks.

USING AI FOR PREDICTIVE ANALYTICS AND PROACTIVE DEFENSE MEASURES

One of the most powerful applications of AI in cybersecurity is its ability to enable **predictive analytics**. Instead of simply responding to threats after they occur, AI can analyze vast amounts of historical and real-time data to predict where and how future attacks might happen. This **proactive defense** approach allows organizations to **preemptively strengthen defenses**, reducing the likelihood of a successful attack.

1. PREDICTIVE ANALYTICS FOR THREAT HUNTING

Threat hunting is a proactive approach to cybersecurity that involves searching for threats before they have a chance to breach defenses. Traditionally, threat hunting has relied on **manual investigation** and **human intuition**, but AI is transforming this process by providing **predictive analytics** that guide threat hunters toward potential vulnerabilities.

- **Analyzing Historical Attack Patterns**:
  AI systems can analyze vast amounts of historical data to identify **patterns** and **trends** in cyberattacks. For example, AI might analyze data from past ransomware attacks to identify common attack vectors, file signatures, and behaviors associated with the initial stages of an attack. Using this knowledge, AI systems can predict which assets are most likely to be targeted in future attacks.
- **Identifying Vulnerabilities**:
  Predictive analytics powered by AI can also be used to identify **vulnerabilities** in an organization's infrastructure. By continuously analyzing system logs, network traffic, and software configurations, AI can highlight **potential weaknesses**—such as unpatched software, exposed ports, or misconfigurations—that attackers could exploit. Once

identified, defenders can proactively address these vulnerabilities, reducing the risk of exploitation.

2. PROACTIVE DEFENSE STRATEGIES

AI enables organizations to adopt **proactive defense strategies** by predicting threats and automatically implementing defensive measures before an attack occurs. These strategies allow cybersecurity teams to stay one step ahead of attackers, minimizing the attack surface and preventing breaches before they happen.

- **Dynamic Patch Management:**
  One key application of AI-driven proactive defense is **dynamic patch management**. AI systems can predict which vulnerabilities are most likely to be exploited based on current threat intelligence and past attack patterns. This allows organizations to prioritize patching efforts, ensuring that the most critical vulnerabilities are addressed before attackers can exploit them.
- **Preemptive Network Segmentation:**
  Another proactive defense strategy enabled by AI is **preemptive network segmentation**. AI can analyze network traffic and automatically segment parts of the network based on risk factors. For instance, if AI predicts that a specific server is at high risk of being targeted due to vulnerabilities, it can automatically move the server to an isolated network segment, reducing the potential impact of an attack.

By leveraging **AI-powered predictive analytics**, organizations can shift from a reactive to a proactive defense posture, identifying and addressing potential threats before they can materialize into full-scale attacks.

Automated Incident Response Through SDN

Software Defined Networking (SDN) is a technology that allows for **dynamic control** of network traffic and infrastructure through software rather than traditional hardware configurations. When combined with AI, SDN can enable **automated incident response** at unprecedented speed and scale, ensuring that threats are contained and neutralized before they can cause significant harm.

1. Dynamic Network Control Through SDN

SDN separates the **control plane** from the **data plane**, allowing network administrators to manage network traffic centrally and dynamically. In the context of cybersecurity, this centralized control enables rapid, automated responses to incidents, such as isolating compromised devices, rerouting traffic, or blocking malicious IP addresses in real-time.

- **Traffic Rerouting**:
  In the event of an attack, such as a **Distributed Denial of Service (DDoS)** or a **ransomware outbreak**, SDN can automatically reroute network traffic to mitigate the impact. For example, if a specific segment of the network is experiencing a DDoS attack, SDN can reroute legitimate traffic through alternative pathways, ensuring that critical services remain operational while blocking malicious traffic.
- **Dynamic Network Segmentation**:
  SDN allows for **dynamic network segmentation**, which is particularly useful in responding to security incidents. AI systems can detect suspicious activity in one part of the network and, using SDN, automatically create isolated segments to quarantine compromised systems. This prevents the spread of malware or lateral movement by attackers, containing the threat to a small portion of the network while the incident is investigated.

2. AI-DRIVEN INCIDENT RESPONSE

When integrated with AI, SDN becomes an even more powerful tool for **automated incident response**. AI systems can analyze **network traffic** and **anomalies** in real-time, making decisions about how to respond based on pre-defined security policies or learned behavior.

- **Real-Time Response**:
  AI-driven SDN can initiate responses to incidents within milliseconds, significantly reducing the time attackers have to exploit vulnerabilities. For example, if AI detects a **phishing attack** or signs of **data exfiltration**, it can use SDN to block outbound traffic from the compromised systems or redirect malicious activity to a honeypot for further analysis.
- **Automated Containment**:
  One of the key benefits of combining AI with SDN is the ability to **automate containment**. AI can dynamically adjust the network environment based on the severity of the threat. For example, if AI detects that an internal system is compromised, SDN can automatically isolate that system, disconnect it from sensitive resources, and initiate a security investigation—all without the need for human intervention.

By leveraging **AI-driven automation** and **SDN**, organizations can implement a highly effective, real-time **incident response system** that minimizes the damage caused by cyberattacks while maintaining operational continuity.

How to Overwhelm Attackers with Guerrilla-Style Attrition Warfare

In traditional warfare, **guerrilla tactics** involve using mobility, deception, and attrition to wear down a larger, more powerful adversary over time. In the context of cybersecurity, these same principles can be applied through **AI-driven automation**, where defenders continually disrupt, deceive, and wear down attackers by forcing them to expend resources and time without gaining any meaningful advantage.

1. CONTINUOUS DEFENSIVE ACTIONS

One of the hallmarks of **guerrilla warfare** is the use of **constant pressure** to wear down an adversary. In cybersecurity, this can be achieved by automating **continuous defensive actions** that disrupt attackers' activities and force them to expend resources trying to overcome the defenses.

- **Automated Deception**:
  AI can be used to create **deceptive environments** such as **honeypots** or **honeynets** that lure attackers into wasting time and resources on decoy systems. By constantly updating and moving these decoys, AI systems can create a shifting landscape that confuses attackers and makes it difficult for them to differentiate between real and fake targets. This forces attackers to spend more time and effort trying to find valuable assets, effectively exhausting their resources.
- **Dynamic Obfuscation**:
  Another way to overwhelm attackers is through **dynamic obfuscation**, where AI systems continuously change the network topology, system configurations, and security settings. This makes it difficult for attackers to map the network or exploit known vulnerabilities, forcing them to constantly adapt their strategies. Over time, this strategy wears down the attacker's ability to maintain a coherent attack plan.

2. ATTRITION THROUGH AUTOMATED RESPONSE

Attrition warfare in cybersecurity involves forcing attackers to expend more resources—time, bandwidth, or computational power—than they can afford to sustain. By using **AI-driven**

automation, defenders can apply constant pressure to attackers, making it difficult for them to achieve their objectives.

- **Automated Attack Mitigation:**
  AI can continuously monitor the environment and apply **mitigation techniques** that degrade the attacker's capabilities. For example, if an attacker is attempting to launch a brute-force attack against a network, AI can automatically slow down or block the attack, forcing the attacker to either increase their resources or abandon the attempt. Over time, this attrition strategy makes the cost of attacking higher than the potential reward.
- **AI-Driven Counterattacks:**
  In some cases, AI can be programmed to **counterattack** by exploiting weaknesses in the attacker's infrastructure. For example, if AI detects that an attacker is using a botnet, it can identify the command-and-control (C2) servers and attempt to disrupt or take them offline. This kind of **guerrilla-style counteroffensive** forces attackers to divert resources to defend their own infrastructure, further diminishing their ability to sustain an attack.

By using **guerrilla-style attrition tactics**, defenders can keep attackers on the defensive, forcing them to expend resources without gaining ground. Over time, this strategy can exhaust even the most persistent adversaries, making it difficult for them to maintain their operations.

CONCLUSION: AI-DRIVEN AUTOMATION AND PROACTIVE DEFENSE IN CYBERSECURITY

As cyberattacks become more **automated** and **sophisticated**, the need for **AI-driven automation** and **proactive defense strategies** has never been greater. By leveraging **AI-powered predictive analytics, SDN**, and **guerrilla-style tactics**, organizations can defend themselves in real-time, outmaneuver attackers, and stay one step ahead of evolving threats.

AI's ability to **automate defense actions**, enable **real-time incident response**, and apply **proactive measures** based on predictive analytics transforms how cybersecurity teams operate, allowing them to act with greater speed and precision. Additionally, by using **attrition warfare tactics**, defenders can continuously disrupt and overwhelm attackers, forcing them to expend valuable resources and ultimately abandon their attempts.

As AI continues to evolve, its role in **cybersecurity automation** will become even more critical, enabling organizations to implement **adaptive**, **resilient**, and **effective defense systems** that can withstand the most sophisticated adversaries.

CHAPTER 16: COLLABORATION WITH NATIONAL CYBERSECURITY AGENCIES AND ALLIES

INTRODUCTION

In an interconnected digital world, **cyber threats** do not respect national borders or organizational boundaries. Nation-state attacks, cyber espionage, and criminal syndicates have the ability to cripple critical infrastructure, steal sensitive data, and disrupt global supply chains. In this environment, no single organization, nation, or sector can adequately defend against the sophisticated and persistent threats that dominate the cybersecurity landscape. The need for **collaboration**—between **national cybersecurity agencies (NCSA)**, **private sector organizations**, and **global allies**—has become a cornerstone of modern cyber defense strategies.

Partnerships at the national and international levels offer enhanced visibility, shared intelligence, and unified responses to cyberattacks. **Public-private collaborations** ensure that information and resources are shared between government bodies and businesses, enhancing mutual protection. **Cyber defense alliances**, with **decentralized command structures** and unified goals, allow for quick and coordinated responses to large-scale cyber incidents.

In this chapter, we will examine how **collaboration with national cybersecurity agencies, public-private partnerships**, and **international alliances** enhance global defense strategies. We will also explore how technologies such as **AI, Software Defined Networking (SDN)**, and **AI-driven access control** can be leveraged to create more dynamic and effective global cyber defenses.

The Power of Partnerships in Cyber Defense

In the realm of cybersecurity, **partnerships** between governments, private sector organizations, and international bodies are crucial for maintaining a strong defense posture. These collaborations offer significant advantages, such as shared threat intelligence, mutual defense protocols, and access to specialized resources that no single entity could deploy on its own.

1. SHARED THREAT INTELLIGENCE

One of the most significant benefits of cybersecurity partnerships is the ability to share **threat intelligence** across borders and sectors. Cyber threats evolve rapidly, and the ability to quickly disseminate information about new attack vectors, malware strains, or vulnerabilities can be the difference between containing a threat and allowing it to spread unchecked.

- **Global Threat Sharing Platforms**:
  Many national cybersecurity agencies, such as the **United**

States Cybersecurity and Infrastructure Security Agency (CISA), the **European Union Agency for Cybersecurity (ENISA)**, and the **UK National Cyber Security Centre (NCSC)**, facilitate platforms where private sector organizations and governments can **share threat intelligence** in real-time. These platforms enable organizations to collaborate on tracking threats, developing defensive strategies, and sharing information on emerging vulnerabilities and best practices.
- **Joint Cyber Exercises**:
Regularly conducted **joint cyber exercises** between national agencies and private sector organizations simulate real-world attack scenarios, allowing partners to test their defenses and improve coordination. These exercises improve **response times**, reveal **gaps in defenses**, and foster collaboration by allowing participants to rehearse roles in global incident response strategies.

2. FASTER AND COORDINATED RESPONSES

In the face of widespread cyberattacks, **coordinated responses** across national and sectoral boundaries are essential. **Ransomware attacks**, **DDoS campaigns**, and **state-sponsored espionage** can quickly overwhelm an isolated organization or nation-state. Partnerships allow for **faster response times**, more **comprehensive defenses**, and **shared mitigation strategies**.

- **Mutual Assistance Agreements**:
Partnerships between governments and organizations often include **mutual assistance agreements**, ensuring that when a cyberattack occurs, resources, expertise, and infrastructure can be shared to mitigate the threat. This is particularly important in critical infrastructure sectors like **energy**, **finance**, and **healthcare**, where the consequences of a successful cyberattack can be devastating.
- **Global Incident Response Teams**:
Many countries have formed **global incident response teams** that include experts from national cybersecurity agencies,

private companies, and international organizations. These teams are tasked with responding to **large-scale incidents** by deploying expertise, forensic capabilities, and resources to help affected organizations recover quickly.

By fostering **partnerships** and **collaboration**, organizations and governments can create a **unified front** that enhances their ability to defend against modern cyber threats, respond to incidents more quickly, and prevent attacks from causing widespread damage.

PUBLIC-PRIVATE SECTOR COLLABORATION FOR STRONGER DEFENSE

In the cyber domain, **public-private sector collaboration** is critical. While governments have access to national security resources and intelligence, the private sector controls the majority of the world's **critical infrastructure** and is often the target of cyberattacks. By collaborating, both sectors can share **resources, expertise,** and **intelligence** to improve overall defense capabilities.

1. GOVERNMENT SUPPORT FOR PRIVATE SECTOR DEFENSE

Governments, through **national cybersecurity agencies (NCSA)**, play a key role in supporting the private sector by providing access to **threat intelligence**, offering **guidance on best practices**, and, in some cases, offering **financial support** for enhancing cybersecurity defenses.

- **Information Sharing and Analysis Centers (ISACs)**: Governments have established **Information Sharing and Analysis Centers (ISACs)** for various critical industries such as finance, healthcare, energy, and transportation. ISACs are platforms where private organizations can **share threat information** with one another and with government agencies. By centralizing this information, ISACs enable

organizations to better understand the threat landscape and respond more effectively to emerging risks.
- **Cybersecurity Grant Programs**:
  Some governments offer **cybersecurity grant programs** that provide funding to private companies, particularly those in critical infrastructure sectors, to help them enhance their security capabilities. These grants are often used to invest in new technologies, such as **AI-driven cybersecurity systems**, and to train personnel in **incident response** and **forensic analysis**.

2. PRIVATE SECTOR INVOLVEMENT IN NATIONAL DEFENSE

The private sector also plays an increasingly important role in **national cybersecurity defense**, often providing **innovative solutions**, **technical expertise**, and **advanced technologies** that complement government efforts.

- **Technology Development and Deployment**:
  Many private companies, particularly in the tech sector, are developing cutting-edge **cyber defense technologies**, such as AI-driven threat detection systems, behavioral analytics platforms, and **automated incident response tools**. Governments often rely on these private sector solutions to bolster national defense systems. For example, private companies might partner with national agencies to deploy **machine learning models** for detecting nation-state threats or develop **cloud-based solutions** that enable better **data protection** across distributed networks.
- **Private Sector Engagement in Cyber Policy**:
  Governments are increasingly consulting private sector leaders when developing **cybersecurity policies** and **regulations**. The private sector brings valuable insights into **emerging technologies, market trends**, and **potential vulnerabilities**. By engaging with private companies, governments can develop more **pragmatic, forward-looking**

policies that address the needs of both national security and private sector innovation.

Public-private collaboration is essential for building a strong, resilient cybersecurity infrastructure. By working together, governments and private companies can enhance their defenses, improve threat detection, and respond more effectively to large-scale cyber incidents.

Cyber Defense Alliances: Decentralized Command Structures and Unified Goals

Cyber defense in the modern era increasingly relies on **alliances** between nations, corporations, and international organizations. These alliances enable a **decentralized command structure**, where member states or organizations maintain control over their own defenses but work toward **unified goals** of global cybersecurity.

1. THE IMPORTANCE OF DECENTRALIZED COMMAND STRUCTURES

In cyber defense, **decentralized command structures** allow for greater **flexibility, adaptability,** and **local control** while still enabling cooperation and coordination on a global scale. This is especially important in the context of **cyber alliances**, where member organizations must maintain their own **sovereignty** while working together toward shared cybersecurity objectives.

- **Interoperability and Coordination:**
  Decentralized command structures rely on **interoperability** between member systems and networks. This means ensuring that **defense protocols, incident response plans,** and **threat intelligence** can be easily shared across borders and organizations. For example, NATO's **Cyber Defense Pledge** encourages member states to enhance the **resilience** of their national networks while ensuring that their defense

systems are interoperable with NATO's collective cyber defense framework.

- **Localized Responses with Global Support**:
  In decentralized structures, individual nations or organizations take the lead in **defending their networks**, but they can call upon **allied support** when needed. For example, if a nation is hit by a **cyberattack**, it can request assistance from allied nations to bolster its defenses, share threat intelligence, or provide forensic capabilities. This model ensures a **quick localized response** with the **backing of global resources**.

2. UNIFIED GOALS IN GLOBAL CYBERSECURITY ALLIANCES

While command structures in cyber alliances may be decentralized, the goals are often **unified**. Cyber defense alliances typically share objectives such as **protecting critical infrastructure, enhancing information sharing**, and **coordinating incident response** to cyberattacks that could have **global implications**.

- **NATO Cyber Defense Policy**:
  NATO's **Cyber Defense Policy** is an example of a unified approach to cybersecurity. While each member state is responsible for its own defenses, the alliance collectively works to protect NATO's networks, share intelligence, and coordinate responses to cyberattacks that target the alliance's operations. This creates a **layered defense system**, where individual states contribute to a broader security framework.
- **Global Cybersecurity Pacts**:
  Initiatives like the **Paris Call for Trust and Security in Cyberspace** bring together **nations, corporations**, and **NGOs** to promote a unified vision for **cyber peace, stability**, and **security**. This includes commitments to protect the **integrity of the internet**, safeguard **critical infrastructure**, and defend against **malicious state-sponsored activity**. These agreements

demonstrate the importance of unified goals in global cybersecurity efforts.

NCSA Across the Globe and How to Build Interaction with Them

National Cybersecurity Agencies (NCSA) play a pivotal role in coordinating cybersecurity defenses within their respective countries. These agencies are responsible for protecting national **critical infrastructure**, ensuring **cyber readiness**, and responding to **cyber incidents**. Building strong **interactions** with these agencies is essential for organizations seeking to enhance their cybersecurity posture and ensure they are aligned with national defense strategies.

1. KEY NATIONAL CYBERSECURITY AGENCIES

Across the globe, there are several prominent **NCSAs** that lead national efforts to protect against cyber threats. These agencies often work closely with the private sector and international partners to enhance their defense capabilities.

- **United States: Cybersecurity and Infrastructure Security Agency (CISA):**
  The **CISA** is a critical component of the U.S. Department of Homeland Security and is responsible for **protecting critical infrastructure, coordinating incident response**, and **facilitating information sharing** between government agencies and the private sector. CISA offers tools such as **Einstein**, a cybersecurity system that monitors and analyzes traffic to and from federal agencies, and works with ISACs to promote broader sectoral collaboration.
- **United Kingdom: National Cyber Security Centre (NCSC):**
  The UK's **NCSC**, a division of GCHQ, is responsible for securing the nation's critical infrastructure, promoting best

practices in cybersecurity, and responding to cyber incidents. The NCSC works closely with private organizations to share threat intelligence and provides guidance through its **Active Cyber Defence (ACD)** program, which helps protect against malware, phishing, and other online threats.
- **European Union Agency for Cybersecurity (ENISA):**
ENISA serves as the cybersecurity agency for the **European Union**, coordinating cybersecurity efforts across member states, facilitating **cross-border incident response**, and promoting best practices in cybersecurity. ENISA also plays a key role in shaping **EU cybersecurity policy** and fostering collaboration with other international organizations.

2. BUILDING INTERACTION WITH NCSAS

For private organizations and other national agencies, building effective relationships with **NCSAs** involves fostering **regular communication, sharing intelligence,** and **participating in collaborative exercises**.

- **Establishing Communication Channels:**
Organizations should establish **direct communication channels** with NCSAs to ensure they have access to the latest **threat intelligence** and guidance. This might include joining **ISACs** or participating in **information-sharing platforms** operated by the NCSA. In the event of a cyber incident, direct communication can help organizations quickly report the attack and receive assistance.
- **Participation in Joint Exercises:**
One of the most effective ways to build relationships with NCSAs is by participating in **joint cybersecurity exercises**. These exercises often simulate real-world cyberattacks, allowing participants to practice their **incident response capabilities**, test **collaborative defenses**, and improve **coordination** between government and private sector partners.

By building strong relationships with **NCSAs**, organizations can ensure they are aligned with national cybersecurity priorities, improve their defenses through collaboration, and receive timely assistance in the event of a major cyber incident.

How AI, SDN, and AI Access Control Enhance Global Defense Strategies

Artificial Intelligence (AI), Software Defined Networking (SDN), and **AI-driven access control** systems are revolutionizing the way national cybersecurity agencies and their global partners approach **cyber defense**. These technologies provide **dynamic, scalable,** and **intelligent defense mechanisms** that can enhance global cybersecurity strategies by improving **response times, visibility,** and **coordination**.

1. AI-DRIVEN THREAT DETECTION AND INTELLIGENCE SHARING

AI's ability to process vast amounts of data in real-time makes it an essential tool for **global threat detection** and **intelligence sharing**. AI-driven systems can analyze traffic patterns, detect anomalies, and identify threats faster and more accurately than human analysts.

- **AI-Driven Global Threat Intelligence Platforms**:
  Many national cybersecurity agencies now rely on **AI-driven threat intelligence platforms** that collect data from various sources, analyze potential threats, and share the intelligence with partners across the globe. These platforms enable real-time detection of **emerging threats** and facilitate **rapid dissemination of information**, ensuring that all partners are aware of new attack vectors and vulnerabilities.

2. SOFTWARE DEFINED NETWORKING (SDN) FOR DYNAMIC DEFENSE

SDN enables cybersecurity teams to **dynamically control** their networks, providing the flexibility to respond to threats in real-time. SDN allows for **dynamic network segmentation, traffic rerouting**, and **automated incident response**, making it a critical component of modern cyber defense strategies.

- **Real-Time Network Segmentation**:
  In global defense strategies, SDN enables agencies to **dynamically segment networks** in response to threats. For example, if a certain network segment is under attack, SDN can quickly isolate that segment, preventing the attacker from moving laterally through the network. This capability is particularly useful in critical infrastructure defense, where **isolation** and **containment** are key to preventing widespread damage.

3. AI ACCESS CONTROL FOR GLOBAL SECURITY

AI-driven access control systems use **machine learning** and **behavioral analytics** to ensure that only authorized users can access sensitive systems and data. These systems continuously monitor user behavior, detecting anomalies that may indicate compromised accounts or insider threats.

- **Continuous Authentication and Global Access Policies**:
  AI-driven access control systems enable **continuous authentication**, where users are regularly re-authenticated based on behavioral data. This reduces the risk of compromised credentials being used in attacks. In a global defense context, AI-driven access control systems can enforce **consistent security policies** across different regions, ensuring that **access to sensitive data** is tightly controlled.

By leveraging **AI, SDN**, and **AI-driven access control**, national cybersecurity agencies and their global allies can enhance **global defense strategies**, improve **coordination**, and respond more effectively to **emerging threats**.

Conclusion: The Future of Cyber Defense Collaboration

As the threat landscape becomes increasingly complex, **collaboration** between **national cybersecurity agencies**, the **private sector**, and **international allies** will remain crucial. By building **strong partnerships**, adopting **decentralized command structures**, and embracing **emerging technologies** like **AI, SDN,** and **AI-driven access control**, organizations can ensure that they are prepared to meet the challenges of **modern cyber defense**.

In the future, the ability to **share intelligence, coordinate defenses,** and **respond quickly** to global threats will be paramount. By fostering **collaboration** and leveraging **advanced technologies**, governments and organizations can work together to build a **resilient, adaptive,** and **unified global defense** capable of countering even the most sophisticated cyber adversaries.

CHAPTER 17: THE PLAYBOOK IN ACTION: REAL-WORLD APPLICATIONS

Introduction

The principles of AI-driven cybersecurity, Software Defined Networking (SDN), and guerrilla cyber tactics have moved from theory to practical application. Today, organizations face increasingly complex cyber threats, including advanced persistent threats (APTs), state-sponsored actors, and sophisticated cybercrime syndicates. To counter these threats, companies are adopting innovative defense strategies combining AI, SDN, and asymmetric tactics to protect their assets.

This chapter explores **verified real-world case studies** from various industries, demonstrating how AI and SDN integration has transformed the ability to respond dynamically to threats. These examples showcase the success of modern cybersecurity approaches in creating proactive, adaptive defenses capable of countering sophisticated attackers.

These real-world applications highlight the power of combining advanced technology and strategy, providing a roadmap for organizations looking to build a proactive, adaptive, and robust defense.

Case Studies: Verified Organizations Applying AI, SDN, And Cyber Tactics

1. ANONYMOUS FINANCIAL INSTITUTION: AI AND SDN FOR THREAT DETECTION AND RESPONSE

In 2019, a **major financial institution** experienced a significant data breach after an attacker exploited a vulnerability in the company's cloud infrastructure to access sensitive customer data.

Challenge:
The institution's security systems faced difficulties detecting and preventing targeted attacks that exploited insider knowledge of cloud infrastructure. Traditional detection systems were ineffective against this sophisticated threat.

Solution:
After the breach, the institution invested in **AI-powered threat**

detection systems and integrated SDN technologies to improve its ability to defend against future threats. AI systems were deployed to continuously analyze network traffic and detect unusual behavior patterns. In tandem, SDN allowed dynamic network segmentation, enabling the institution to isolate compromised systems and reroute traffic in real time.

Outcome:
The combination of AI and SDN improved the institution's defenses by enabling faster detection and containment of cyber threats. This led to enhanced protection of sensitive financial data and a reduction in downtime during security incidents.

2. ANONYMOUS HEALTHCARE PROVIDER: DYNAMIC DEFENSE AGAINST RANSOMWARE

A large **healthcare provider** fell victim to a ransomware attack that encrypted critical systems and threatened patient safety by disrupting healthcare services.

Challenge:
The healthcare provider's outdated systems were vulnerable to ransomware attacks, which bypassed traditional defenses and swiftly encrypted essential files, making patient care services inaccessible.

Solution:
In response to the attack, the provider adopted an AI-driven defense strategy. AI-based systems were deployed to monitor internal network traffic and identify irregularities, such as unusual encryption activity or changes in file access patterns. **SDN** was used to isolate infected systems and ensure continuity of care by rerouting traffic to unaffected servers. The organization also used honeypots to divert attackers from real systems, allowing security teams to analyze the malware's behavior.

Outcome:
The integration of AI-driven detection and SDN-based segmentation

allowed the healthcare provider to quickly contain ransomware incidents, preventing further spread across its network. This approach minimized service disruptions and protected patient data without paying any ransom.

3. ANONYMOUS TECHNOLOGY FIRM: ASYMMETRIC DEFENSE AGAINST NATION-STATE ACTORS

A **global technology firm** became the target of a nation-state cyber-espionage campaign, where attackers attempted to steal intellectual property and access customer data.

Challenge:
The attackers employed spear-phishing, social engineering, and custom malware to bypass the firm's traditional defenses. The organization needed to defend against the advanced tactics used by well-resourced nation-state actors.

Solution:
The firm adopted a **guerrilla cyber warfare strategy**, using **AI-driven behavioral analytics** to continuously monitor user activities and detect insider threats or compromised accounts. SDN allowed dynamic network segmentation, limiting the movement of attackers within the network and protecting sensitive areas. The firm also used automated decoy systems to mislead attackers into targeting fake assets, giving security teams more time to respond.

Outcome:
By combining AI, SDN, and guerrilla tactics, the technology firm successfully thwarted the nation-state attack. The attackers were unable to access valuable intellectual property, and the security team gathered useful intelligence about the attackers' methods.

EXAMPLES OF SDN AND AI INTEGRATION FOR DYNAMIC DEFENSE

1. ANONYMOUS CLOUD PROVIDER: AI-DRIVEN CLOUD SECURITY

A **major cloud infrastructure provider** integrated AI and SDN to protect its massive environment from cyber threats, ensuring the security of customer data and continuous uptime.

Challenge:
The provider faced frequent cyber threats, including DDoS attacks and insider threats, targeting its clients' data and infrastructure. Managing security for a cloud environment serving thousands of clients required real-time threat detection and a scalable defense solution.

Solution:
The provider implemented **AI-driven security tools** to analyze network traffic for unusual behavior, such as sudden spikes in login attempts or abnormal data flows. Using **SDN**, the company dynamically reconfigured its network in response to threats, isolating compromised areas and rerouting traffic to unaffected regions.

Outcome:
AI and SDN integration enabled the cloud provider to quickly detect and mitigate security threats while maintaining the performance of its infrastructure. The solution ensured that client data remained secure and prevented major service disruptions.

2. ANONYMOUS INDUSTRIAL MANUFACTURER: SDN IN INDUSTRIAL IOT NETWORKS

A global **industrial manufacturing company** integrated SDN into its Industrial Internet of Things (IIoT) networks to safeguard its critical infrastructure from cyberattacks.

Challenge:
The company's distributed industrial systems were vulnerable to network-based attacks that could disrupt production lines and damage critical equipment.

Solution:
The company deployed **SDN** to create dynamically segmented networks across its factories and production lines. This approach allowed for real-time isolation of any compromised devices or networks. The organization also used **AI-based monitoring** to detect abnormal traffic patterns or unauthorized communications between IoT devices, enabling rapid response to potential breaches.

Outcome:
By integrating SDN and AI, the manufacturer protected its production processes from cyberattacks, preventing disruptions and ensuring that its critical infrastructure operated without interference. This allowed the company to maintain operational continuity in a highly interconnected industrial environment.

3. ANONYMOUS E-COMMERCE PLATFORM: AI-SDN INTEGRATION FOR TRAFFIC MANAGEMENT

An **e-commerce platform** faced traffic surges during seasonal sales events, which made the platform vulnerable to DDoS attacks and performance bottlenecks.

Challenge:
During high-demand periods, the e-commerce platform experienced an overwhelming number of user requests, creating a potential point of failure where attackers could launch DDoS attacks or exploit system vulnerabilities.

Solution:
The company deployed **AI-driven load balancing** to predict traffic spikes and allocate resources accordingly. **SDN** was used to dynamically reroute network traffic and isolate any attempts at

DDoS attacks, ensuring that legitimate traffic continued to flow. The combination of AI and SDN allowed the platform to scale resources in real time, minimizing the impact of malicious traffic.

Outcome:
The AI-SDN integration helped the e-commerce platform maintain uptime during peak traffic periods and mitigated the risk of DDoS attacks. This ensured a seamless customer experience and protected the platform from revenue loss during critical sales events.

CONCLUSION: APPLYING THE PLAYBOOK FOR DYNAMIC AND PROACTIVE DEFENSE

These verified case studies demonstrate how organizations across industries are successfully applying AI, SDN, and asymmetric defense tactics to secure their networks. From finance and healthcare to technology and manufacturing, these real-world examples show the power of combining advanced technologies with adaptive strategies to defend against sophisticated cyber threats.

CHAPTER 18: BLOCKCHAIN IN CYBERSECURITY BASED ON GUERRILLA TACTICS

INTRODUCTION

Blockchain technology, best known for its use in **cryptocurrencies,** is emerging as a powerful tool for **cybersecurity.** Its inherent characteristics—**decentralization, immutability, transparency,** and **security**—make it an ideal solution for defending against increasingly sophisticated cyber threats. As organizations seek new ways to **secure data, protect IoT devices,** and **manage identities,** blockchain offers a decentralized framework that aligns with the principles of **guerrilla warfare tactics** in cybersecurity.

In traditional **guerrilla warfare**, smaller forces use **asymmetry, mobility**, and **decentralization** to counter larger, more powerful adversaries. In the cyber domain, blockchain technology provides similar advantages. By distributing data across a network of nodes, blockchain eliminates single points of failure, making it difficult for attackers to compromise the entire system. Moreover, blockchain's **cryptographic** foundations and **immutable ledgers** ensure that data remains secure and resistant to tampering.

This chapter will explore how **blockchain** can be leveraged for **secure data transmission, decentralized identity management**, and **IoT device protection**. We will also examine **real-world use cases** of blockchain in **supply chain security** and **financial transactions**. Finally, we will discuss how blockchain enables **cyber guerrilla tactics** by decentralizing cyber defense, creating a more resilient and adaptive security infrastructure.

BLOCKCHAIN FOR SECURE DATA TRANSMISSION

In an era where data breaches and cyberattacks are increasingly common, ensuring the **security of data transmission** has become a top priority for organizations. **Blockchain technology** offers a robust solution for **secure data transmission** by providing a **tamper-resistant** and **decentralized** framework that protects data from interception and unauthorized access.

1. Immutable and Transparent Ledger

One of the key features of blockchain is its **immutable ledger**, which records transactions in a secure and transparent manner. Once data is written to the blockchain, it cannot be altered or deleted without consensus from the network, making it highly resistant to tampering.

- **Cryptographic Hashing**:
  Every block in a blockchain contains a cryptographic hash of

the previous block, creating an unbreakable chain of data. This ensures that any attempt to alter a single block would require altering all subsequent blocks, which is computationally infeasible in a properly secured blockchain. This immutability is crucial for **secure data transmission**, as it guarantees the **integrity** and **authenticity** of the data being transmitted.

- **End-to-End Encryption**:
  Blockchain can be combined with **end-to-end encryption** to ensure that data remains secure during transmission. Each transaction or data exchange on the blockchain is encrypted using cryptographic algorithms, making it impossible for unauthorized parties to read the data without the appropriate decryption key. This makes blockchain an ideal solution for **secure communications** between parties in **sensitive industries** such as finance, healthcare, and defense.

2. Decentralization Eliminates Single Points of Failure

One of the major weaknesses in traditional centralized systems is the existence of **single points of failure**—centralized servers or databases that, if compromised, can give attackers access to large amounts of sensitive data. Blockchain's **decentralized architecture** eliminates this vulnerability by distributing data across a network of nodes, making it much harder for attackers to target a single point of failure.

- **Resilience Against Attacks**:
  In a decentralized blockchain network, data is stored and replicated across multiple nodes, ensuring that even if one or several nodes are compromised, the integrity of the entire network remains intact. This resilience is key in **cyber guerrilla tactics**, as it enables defenders to maintain security even in the face of concerted attacks on individual components of the system.

- **Peer-to-Peer Secure Transmission**:
  Blockchain facilitates **peer-to-peer** communication without the need for intermediaries, reducing the risk of interception by malicious actors. By relying on distributed consensus protocols, blockchain ensures that data can be transmitted securely between parties without relying on centralized authorities, which are often targets for attackers.

Incorporating blockchain into **secure data transmission** strategies ensures that data is transmitted **securely, tamper-proof**, and resistant to attacks, aligning with guerrilla tactics that focus on **distributed defenses** and **asymmetric advantage**.

DECENTRALIZED IDENTITY MANAGEMENT AND AUTHENTICATION

Identity management and **authentication** are fundamental aspects of cybersecurity, particularly in an environment where **phishing, credential theft**, and **identity spoofing** are among the most common attack vectors. Traditional identity management systems are often centralized and vulnerable to breaches, which can lead to the mass compromise of user credentials. **Blockchain technology**, with its decentralized nature, offers a more **secure** and **resilient** alternative.

1. Self-Sovereign Identity (SSI)

One of the most promising applications of blockchain in identity management is the concept of **self-sovereign identity (SSI)**, which allows individuals to maintain full control over their digital identities without relying on centralized identity providers. In a **self-sovereign identity** system, individuals store their identity data on a blockchain, and they can selectively disclose pieces of that data as needed to prove their identity.

- **Decentralized Identity Verification**:
  Blockchain enables decentralized verification of identities by

allowing third parties to **cryptographically verify** identity claims without having access to the underlying data. For example, a government agency or university can issue a **digital credential** that is stored on a blockchain. When the individual needs to prove their identity or qualifications, they can provide a verifiable claim that the recipient can check against the blockchain for authenticity.

- **Privacy and Control:**
  With **self-sovereign identity,** individuals maintain **full control** over their identity data, deciding who has access to it and under what conditions. This reduces the risk of large-scale data breaches, as there is no centralized database of sensitive identity information for attackers to target. Additionally, blockchain's **cryptographic features** ensure that identity data is securely stored and transmitted.

2. Decentralized Authentication

Traditional **authentication systems**, such as password-based logins, are vulnerable to a wide range of attacks, including **brute force, credential stuffing**, and **phishing**. Blockchain offers a decentralized alternative to traditional authentication mechanisms, allowing for **passwordless** and **multi-factor authentication** (MFA) that is more secure and resistant to attacks.

- **Blockchain-Based Authentication Protocols:**
  Blockchain can be used to create **decentralized authentication protocols** that do not rely on passwords. For example, blockchain-based **public key infrastructure (PKI)** can replace password-based logins with **cryptographic keys** stored on the blockchain. When a user attempts to log in, the system can verify their identity by checking their public key against the blockchain, eliminating the need for passwords.
- **Multi-Factor Authentication with Blockchain:**
  Blockchain can also be integrated with **multi-factor authentication** (MFA) systems to enhance security. In a

blockchain-based MFA system, each factor of authentication (such as a hardware token, biometric data, or a mobile device) is verified on the blockchain. This ensures that even if one factor is compromised, attackers cannot gain access without satisfying all authentication requirements.

By leveraging blockchain for **identity management** and **authentication**, organizations can create a more secure and **decentralized identity system**, reducing the risk of identity theft and unauthorized access while giving users greater control over their personal data.

BLOCKCHAIN'S ROLE IN PROTECTING IoT DEVICES

The proliferation of **Internet of Things (IoT)** devices has introduced new challenges for cybersecurity, as many IoT devices lack robust security features and are vulnerable to exploitation. **Blockchain technology** can play a critical role in securing IoT devices by providing a **decentralized framework** for managing **device authentication**, **data integrity**, and **communication security**.

1. Decentralized IoT Security Frameworks

Traditional IoT security frameworks often rely on **centralized control** and **device management systems**, which are vulnerable to attacks. By applying blockchain technology, IoT devices can be integrated into a **decentralized network** where security is distributed across all nodes, reducing the risk of a single point of failure.

- **Device Authentication with Blockchain:**
  Blockchain can be used to create a decentralized **device authentication** system for IoT networks. Each IoT device is assigned a unique **cryptographic identifier** stored on the blockchain. When a device attempts to connect to the network, its identity can be verified against the blockchain,

ensuring that only authorized devices can communicate with the network. This prevents attackers from spoofing or impersonating IoT devices.
- **Immutable Data Logs for IoT**:
  IoT devices often generate large volumes of data, which can be vulnerable to tampering or alteration. Blockchain's **immutable ledger** can be used to store data generated by IoT devices, ensuring that the data remains **tamper-proof** and can be traced back to its source. This is particularly important for industries such as **healthcare** and **manufacturing**, where the integrity of IoT data is critical for decision-making.

2. Secure Data Transmission in IoT Networks

Blockchain can also enhance the **security of data transmission** between IoT devices by enabling **peer-to-peer communication** without the need for intermediaries. In a blockchain-enabled IoT network, devices can **securely communicate** with each other using **cryptographically signed transactions**.

- **Reducing the Risk of Man-in-the-Middle Attacks**:
  One of the key advantages of blockchain in IoT security is its ability to prevent **man-in-the-middle (MITM) attacks**. Since all communications between IoT devices are verified using cryptographic hashes and stored on a public ledger, attackers cannot intercept or alter the data without being detected.
- **Energy-Efficient IoT Security**:
  Traditional security protocols for IoT devices, such as **TLS/SSL encryption**, can be resource-intensive and may not be suitable for low-power devices. Blockchain offers a more **energy-efficient** solution, as devices can communicate securely using lightweight cryptographic signatures, reducing the computational overhead required for encryption.

By using blockchain to secure IoT devices, organizations can create a more **resilient** and **decentralized IoT network**, ensuring that devices are **authenticated** and **data transmission** is secure.

Use Cases: Supply Chain Security and Financial Transactions

Blockchain technology is already being deployed in real-world applications, particularly in industries such as **supply chain management** and **financial services**, where **security, transparency,** and **trust** are critical.

1. Blockchain for Supply Chain Security

Supply chain security is one of the most promising use cases for blockchain technology. In complex global supply chains, ensuring the **authenticity** and **integrity** of products as they move through multiple parties is a significant challenge. Blockchain provides a **transparent** and **immutable record** of every transaction and movement within the supply chain, enabling all parties to **track products** from origin to delivery.

- **Traceability and Accountability**:
  In a blockchain-enabled supply chain, each product is assigned a **unique digital identifier** that is recorded on the blockchain. As the product moves through various stages of the supply chain, each transaction is recorded on the blockchain, providing a **complete audit trail** of the product's journey. This ensures that counterfeit or tampered products can be quickly identified, and all parties can be held accountable for their role in the supply chain.
- **Preventing Counterfeiting**:
  Blockchain can also help combat **counterfeiting** by providing a secure and **tamper-proof system** for verifying the authenticity of products. For example, luxury goods manufacturers can use blockchain to assign **digital certificates of authenticity** to their products, which can be verified by consumers or retailers by checking the blockchain.

2. Blockchain in Financial Transactions

Blockchain's role in **financial transactions** is well-established, with **cryptocurrencies** like Bitcoin and Ethereum providing decentralized alternatives to traditional financial systems. However, blockchain's potential in **financial cybersecurity** extends beyond cryptocurrencies.

- **Secure Cross-Border Transactions**:
  Blockchain can facilitate **secure cross-border financial transactions** without the need for intermediaries such as banks or clearinghouses. By using **smart contracts**, blockchain enables **automated transactions** that are executed only when predefined conditions are met, reducing the risk of fraud or manipulation.
- **Preventing Financial Fraud**:
  Blockchain's **immutable ledger** makes it highly effective for preventing **financial fraud**. Every transaction on the blockchain is permanently recorded, making it impossible for bad actors to alter transaction histories or engage in fraudulent activities without being detected.

These use cases demonstrate blockchain's potential to revolutionize **supply chain security** and **financial transactions**, providing enhanced **transparency**, **trust**, and **security** in industries that rely on secure data transmission and transaction integrity.

GUERRILLA TACTICS WITH BLOCKCHAIN: DECENTRALIZING CYBER DEFENSE

Blockchain technology aligns closely with the principles of **cyber guerrilla warfare**, which emphasizes **asymmetry**, **decentralization**, and **resilience**. By decentralizing key aspects of cybersecurity, blockchain enables organizations to defend themselves against more powerful adversaries, such as **nation-state actors** or **well-funded cybercriminals**.

1. Decentralizing Cyber Defense

In traditional cybersecurity models, **centralized systems** are often the target of cyberattacks. By decentralizing critical infrastructure using blockchain, organizations can distribute security responsibilities across a **network of nodes**, making it much harder for attackers to compromise the entire system.

- **Resilience Through Decentralization**:
  Blockchain's decentralized nature ensures that even if part of the network is compromised, the rest of the system remains secure. This is a key **guerrilla tactic**, as it allows defenders to withstand attacks by distributing resources and eliminating single points of failure.
- **Peer-to-Peer Security Models**:
  Blockchain enables **peer-to-peer security models**, where security decisions are made collectively by the network rather than by a central authority. This makes it more difficult for attackers to target a specific decision-maker or authority, further enhancing the resilience of the defense system.

2. Using Blockchain for Offensive Cyber Defense

In addition to its defensive applications, blockchain can also be used as an **offensive tool** in cyber defense strategies. For example, blockchain-based systems can be used to **trap** or **mislead attackers** by creating decoy networks that mimic real systems.

- **Blockchain Honeypots**:
  Defenders can deploy **blockchain honeypots** that lure attackers into targeting **deceptive systems**. These honeypots can be designed to resemble high-value targets, such as **cryptocurrency wallets** or **sensitive data repositories**, but are in fact part of a decoy network. Once attackers engage with the honeypot, defenders can gather intelligence on their tactics and techniques.
- **Blockchain-Enabled Attribution**:
  One of the challenges in cyber warfare is accurately

attributing attacks to specific actors. Blockchain's **transparent ledger** can be used to **track and attribute** the actions of attackers, providing a **forensic trail** that can be used to identify the source of an attack. By using blockchain to monitor and log attacker activity, defenders can gain valuable insights into their adversaries.

CONCLUSION: LEVERAGING BLOCKCHAIN FOR CYBER GUERRILLA WARFARE

As **cyber threats** become more sophisticated, **blockchain technology** offers a powerful tool for decentralizing and strengthening **cyber defenses**. By leveraging blockchain's **immutability, transparency**, and **decentralization**, organizations can create more **resilient defense systems** that align with the principles of **guerrilla warfare**. Whether it's securing **data transmission**, protecting **IoT devices**, or ensuring the **integrity of financial transactions**, blockchain provides a decentralized framework that makes it harder for attackers to succeed.

Incorporating **blockchain** into **cyber guerrilla tactics** allows defenders to **decentralize security**, eliminate **single points of failure**, and create an adaptive and **self-healing defense infrastructure** capable of withstanding even the most persistent cyber threats.

CHAPTER 19: QUANTUM COMPUTING: A DOUBLE-EDGED SWORD

Introduction

Quantum computing represents one of the most revolutionary technological advancements on the horizon, capable of solving complex problems far faster than traditional computers. Its ability to manipulate **qubits** (quantum bits) allows for **parallel processing** of information on a massive scale, potentially solving problems that are intractable for classical computers. While this quantum revolution promises breakthroughs in fields such as drug discovery, materials science, and artificial intelligence, it also poses a significant **double-edged sword** for the field of cybersecurity.

On one hand, **quantum computing** threatens the very foundation of **modern cryptographic systems**—encryption methods that currently secure the world's communications, financial transactions, and government secrets. On the other hand, quantum technology could also provide **new defensive capabilities**, enabling faster, more secure communications and the potential for new types of cryptographic systems designed to withstand quantum attacks.

This chapter will examine the **threats** posed by quantum computing to cryptography, explore the emergence of **post-quantum cryptography**, and discuss how **quantum-assisted cyber defense** could provide benefits for cybersecurity. We will also delve into the **quantum-resistant algorithms** that will protect future systems and explore how quantum technologies can be integrated into **guerrilla cyber defense** strategies to outmaneuver attackers in a quantum-enabled world.

Quantum Computing and Its Threat to Cryptography

The primary threat quantum computing poses to cybersecurity comes from its ability to **break classical cryptographic systems**. Most modern encryption relies on the difficulty of solving certain mathematical problems—such as factoring large integers or computing discrete logarithms—that classical computers cannot solve efficiently. However, **quantum computers** can solve these problems exponentially faster, undermining the **public-key cryptographic algorithms** that protect most of today's communications.

1. Shor's Algorithm and the Breaking of RSA

In 1994, **Peter Shor** developed a quantum algorithm—now known as Shor's Algorithm—which can efficiently factor large numbers and solve **discrete logarithm problems**. These problems are the mathematical foundations of widely-used cryptographic systems such as **RSA, Diffie-Hellman**, and **Elliptic Curve Cryptography (ECC)**.

- **The Threat to RSA Encryption**:
  RSA encryption relies on the difficulty of factoring the product of two large prime numbers. For classical computers, factoring a number that is the product of two primes with several hundred digits would take an impractically long time. However, a quantum computer running **Shor's Algorithm** could solve this problem exponentially faster, rendering RSA encryption effectively **obsolete** once large-scale quantum computers become a reality.
- **Impact on Secure Communications**:
  RSA is widely used in **secure communications**, including protocols like **SSL/TLS** (used for HTTPS websites) and **VPN encryption**. If quantum computers can break RSA, they could decrypt sensitive communications, steal financial information, and compromise state secrets.

2. Grover's Algorithm and Symmetric Encryption

Quantum computers also pose a threat to **symmetric-key encryption algorithms**, though the impact is less severe than with public-key systems. **Grover's Algorithm** is another quantum algorithm that can search through unsorted databases much faster than classical algorithms. This can be applied to **brute-force attacks** on symmetric encryption systems, such as **AES (Advanced Encryption Standard)**.

- **Doubling the Key Size**:
  While Grover's Algorithm provides a **quadratic speedup** for breaking symmetric-key encryption, it doesn't break these systems completely. In practice, to maintain the same level of security in a quantum world, organizations will need to **double the key size** of their encryption algorithms. For example, **AES-256** (with a 256-bit key) is expected to be resistant to quantum attacks, while **AES-128** would no longer provide sufficient security.

The advent of **large-scale quantum computers** will make today's encryption standards vulnerable, forcing organizations to transition to **quantum-safe alternatives** that can withstand the processing power of quantum machines.

Post-Quantum Cryptography: The Next Frontier in Defense

Given the threat posed by quantum computing to current cryptographic systems, researchers are working on developing **post-quantum cryptography (PQC)**—new cryptographic algorithms designed to resist attacks from quantum computers. These algorithms must provide the same level of security as current cryptographic standards but must be based on mathematical problems that are **intractable** for both classical and quantum computers.

1. Lattice-Based Cryptography

One of the most promising candidates for **post-quantum cryptography is lattice-based cryptography**. Lattice-based schemes rely on the hardness of solving certain problems related to **lattice structures**—a complex grid-like arrangement of points in space.

These problems, such as the **Learning with Errors (LWE)** and **Ring Learning with Errors (Ring-LWE)**, are believed to be resistant to quantum attacks.

- **Practical Applications of Lattice Cryptography**:
  Lattice-based cryptography is not only resistant to quantum attacks but also offers additional advantages, such as enabling **fully homomorphic encryption**, which allows computations to be performed on encrypted data without needing to decrypt it first. This could revolutionize fields such as **cloud computing** and **data privacy**, where sensitive data must be processed securely.

2. Code-Based Cryptography

Code-based cryptography is another candidate for post-quantum cryptography, relying on the hardness of decoding **random linear codes**. The **McEliece cryptosystem**, developed in 1978, is a well-known example of a code-based encryption scheme that is believed to be quantum-resistant.

- **McEliece and Durability**:
  The **McEliece cryptosystem** has withstood decades of cryptanalysis and is considered secure against both classical and quantum attacks. Its main drawback is the relatively large size of the public and private keys, but ongoing research aims to reduce these key sizes to make the system more practical for widespread use.

3. Multivariate and Hash-Based Cryptography

Other promising post-quantum cryptographic approaches include **multivariate cryptography**, which involves solving systems of multivariate polynomial equations, and **hash-based cryptography**, which relies on the security of **cryptographic hash functions**.

- **Hash-Based Signatures**:
  Hash-based signature schemes are particularly well-suited for quantum resistance because they are based on well-understood cryptographic hash functions like **SHA-256**, which are not easily broken by quantum algorithms. These signature schemes can be used to verify the integrity of digital communications in a post-quantum world.

As quantum computers become more powerful, **post-quantum cryptography** will become the standard for protecting sensitive data and securing communications. Organizations must start preparing for the transition to **quantum-resistant algorithms** before quantum computers become a threat.

Quantum-Assisted Cyber Defense: Potential Benefits

While quantum computing poses significant challenges to cybersecurity, it also offers opportunities to enhance **cyber defense** through **quantum-assisted technologies**. Quantum computers can perform certain tasks that are **computationally prohibitive** for classical computers, providing defenders with new tools to **detect, analyze**, and **respond** to cyber threats more efficiently.

1. Quantum Machine Learning for Cybersecurity

One of the most promising applications of quantum computing in cybersecurity is the use of **quantum machine learning** (QML) to improve threat detection and response. Quantum computers can process and analyze **large datasets** far more quickly than classical systems, making them ideal for detecting **anomalies** in network traffic, **predicting attack vectors**, and **classifying malware**.

- Faster Anomaly Detection:
  Quantum machine learning can be used to **train models** that detect anomalies in network traffic at a much faster rate

than classical machine learning systems. This enables cybersecurity teams to identify and respond to **zero-day attacks** and other advanced threats before they cause significant damage.

- **Quantum-Assisted Threat Intelligence**:
Quantum computing can also accelerate the processing of **threat intelligence** by analyzing vast amounts of data from **threat feeds, social media**, and **dark web sources**. This enables real-time **threat detection** and more effective responses to cyber incidents.

2. Quantum-Enhanced Cryptography

While quantum computers pose a threat to classical cryptographic systems, they also offer the potential for **quantum-enhanced cryptography**. For example, **Quantum Key Distribution (QKD)** allows two parties to securely exchange encryption keys using the principles of quantum mechanics.

- **Unbreakable Encryption with QKD**:
Quantum Key Distribution provides a method of secure communication that is **provably secure** against eavesdropping. Any attempt to intercept the quantum key exchange would disturb the quantum state of the particles, alerting the parties to the presence of an attacker. This makes **QKD** a powerful tool for **high-security communications**, such as in **military, government**, and **financial sectors**.

As quantum technology matures, its ability to **enhance cybersecurity** through **quantum-assisted defense systems** and **quantum-enhanced encryption** will become increasingly important.

QUANTUM-RESISTANT ALGORITHMS FOR CYBERSECURITY

The development of **quantum-resistant algorithms** is essential for ensuring the long-term security of digital systems in the face of quantum computing. These algorithms are designed to withstand attacks from quantum computers while maintaining performance and scalability.

1. Transitioning to Quantum-Resistant Cryptography

To prepare for the quantum era, organizations must begin the process of transitioning from current cryptographic algorithms to **quantum-resistant alternatives**. This transition will be a complex, multi-year effort that involves updating **cryptographic libraries**, reconfiguring **protocols**, and securing **supply chains** to ensure that data remains protected against future quantum attacks.

- **NIST Post-Quantum Cryptography Standardization:**
  The **National Institute of Standards and Technology (NIST)** is leading the effort to standardize **post-quantum cryptographic algorithms**. In recent years, NIST has been evaluating candidate algorithms that offer strong security against quantum attacks, with the goal of establishing a suite of **quantum-safe cryptographic standards**. Organizations should follow NIST's recommendations and begin preparing to adopt these algorithms as they are standardized.

2. Quantum-Resistant VPNs and Secure Communication Protocols

Virtual Private Networks (VPNs) and **secure communication protocols** will need to be updated with **quantum-resistant cryptographic algorithms** to ensure that sensitive data can be securely transmitted in a post-quantum world.

- **Quantum-Safe VPN Solutions:**
  Several vendors are already developing **quantum-safe VPN solutions** that integrate post-quantum cryptography with

existing network security protocols. These solutions will allow organizations to continue using VPNs for secure communications while ensuring that the data remains protected from quantum-enabled attackers.

3. Quantum-Resistant Blockchain Technologies

Blockchain technology, which relies on **cryptographic algorithms** for securing transactions, will also need to adapt to the quantum era. Researchers are exploring **quantum-resistant blockchain protocols** that use post-quantum cryptographic algorithms to ensure the integrity and security of decentralized ledgers.

- **Post-Quantum Signatures for Blockchain:**
  Digital signatures used in blockchain protocols, such as **Elliptic Curve Digital Signature Algorithm (ECDSA)**, are vulnerable to quantum attacks. Quantum-resistant signature schemes, such as **lattice-based signatures** or **hash-based signatures**, will need to be integrated into blockchain systems to maintain the security of decentralized applications.

The development and adoption of **quantum-resistant algorithms** are critical for ensuring the long-term security of our digital infrastructure in the face of quantum computing.

FUTURE USE OF QUANTUM IN GUERRILLA CYBER DEFENSE

The principles of **guerrilla warfare**, which emphasize **asymmetry, mobility**, and **deception**, can be applied to **quantum-enhanced cyber defense** strategies. In a quantum-enabled world, defenders can leverage quantum technologies to create **dynamic, resilient** defense systems that outmaneuver attackers.

1. Quantum Deception and Attrition Warfare

In **guerrilla cyber defense**, **deception** and **attrition** are key tactics for wearing down a more powerful adversary. Quantum technology offers new opportunities for enhancing these tactics in the cyber domain.

- **Quantum Decoys and Honeypots**:
  Quantum decoys and **honeypots** can be used to mislead attackers into expending their resources on false targets. These decoys could be designed to mimic **high-value cryptographic keys** or **sensitive communications**, tricking quantum attackers into chasing **false leads** while the real systems remain secure. By forcing attackers to waste their quantum computing power on decoys, defenders can **exhaust** their resources and **delay their progress**, a key principle of **attrition warfare**.
- **Quantum-Enhanced Honeynets**:
  In a **quantum-enhanced honeynet**, defenders could deploy **quantum-simulated environments** that appear indistinguishable from real networks to an attacker. These honeynets would allow defenders to observe quantum-enabled attacks in real time while preventing any actual damage to the organization's critical infrastructure. This provides valuable intelligence on **quantum attack methods** and helps defenders improve their quantum-resistant defenses.

2. Dynamic Quantum-Assisted Defense Systems

The **mobility** and **adaptability** emphasized in **guerrilla tactics** can also be enhanced by quantum technology. **Quantum-assisted defense systems** could provide real-time reconfiguration of networks, ensuring that defenders stay ahead of attackers in a constantly shifting cyber battlefield.

- **Quantum-Secure Communication Networks**:
  Using **Quantum Key Distribution (QKD)**, defenders can establish **secure communication channels** that are immune

to interception. This is particularly valuable in **military** and **intelligence** operations, where secure communications are critical to the success of guerrilla tactics. With QKD, defenders can continuously **rotate encryption keys** and dynamically **reconfigure networks** to avoid detection and interception by adversaries.

- **Quantum-Assisted Threat Intelligence**:
  By leveraging quantum computing to process **threat intelligence** faster, defenders can stay ahead of quantum-enabled attackers. **Real-time quantum-assisted analysis** of global threat intelligence feeds would allow defenders to predict attack patterns and preemptively adapt their defenses.

The future of **guerrilla cyber defense** will be defined by the ability to integrate **quantum technologies** into **dynamic, adaptive defense strategies** that exploit the weaknesses of more powerful adversaries.

Conclusion: Navigating the Quantum Frontier in Cyber Defense

As we stand on the cusp of the **quantum revolution**, the dual nature of **quantum computing** as both a threat and a potential asset to cybersecurity becomes clear. On one hand, quantum computers pose a **serious threat** to the cryptographic systems that secure modern communications and data. On the other hand, quantum technology offers new tools for **enhancing cyber defense**, from **quantum-resistant cryptography** to **quantum-assisted threat detection**.

Organizations must begin preparing for the **quantum era** by adopting **post-quantum cryptographic algorithms**, securing IoT devices, and investing in **quantum-safe communications**. Meanwhile, defenders can leverage **quantum technologies** to enhance their **guerrilla** warfare tactics, using **deception**, **mobility**, and **attrition** to outmaneuver attackers in an ever-changing cyber battlefield.

The future of **cyber defense** will be shaped by how effectively we navigate this **quantum frontier**, balancing the **risks** and **opportunities** that quantum computing presents.

CHAPTER 20: EMERGING TECHNOLOGIES: INTEGRATING THE FUTURE INTO CYBER DEFENSE

INTRODUCTION

As the world moves further into the age of **emerging technologies**, the integration of **5G networks**, the **Internet of Things (IoT)**, **cloud computing**, and **autonomous systems** into everyday infrastructure will create new opportunities and challenges for cybersecurity. For defenders, leveraging these technologies will be critical to developing **proactive**, **adaptive**, and **asymmetric defense strategies** grounded in **guerrilla warfare tactics**—a method of defense that focuses on **mobility**, **surprise**, and **attrition** to outmaneuver more powerful adversaries.

Predictive analytics, powered by **AI**, will allow defenders to anticipate attacks before they occur, while **5G networks** and the expansion of **IoT devices** will introduce significant cybersecurity risks due to the expanded attack surface. At the same time, **cloud security** will need to adapt, incorporating **AI** and **blockchain** to enhance protection for distributed systems. The rise of **autonomous systems** will further reshape the battlefield, as both attackers and defenders deploy **autonomous cyber tools** to automate and scale their operations.

This chapter explores how defenders can integrate these emerging technologies into **cyber guerrilla warfare tactics**, providing **case studies** and **practical examples** of how predictive analytics, 5G, IoT, cloud security, and autonomous systems can be used to **proactively defend** against advanced threats.

PREDICTIVE ANALYTICS AND PROACTIVE CYBERSECURITY STRATEGIES

Predictive analytics involves the use of **machine learning** and AI to analyze historical data and make predictions about future outcomes. In the context of cybersecurity, predictive analytics enables organizations to anticipate and mitigate cyber threats before they can cause significant damage. By leveraging **proactive defense strategies**, defenders can outmaneuver attackers, neutralizing threats before they reach their targets.

1. The Role of AI in Predictive Analytics for Cybersecurity

Predictive analytics relies heavily on **AI-driven data analysis** to identify patterns and trends in **network traffic**, **user behavior**, and **threat intelligence**. By continuously analyzing data from various sources, AI systems can detect early warning signs of an impending attack and suggest **preemptive actions** to mitigate the threat.

- **Behavioral Analytics**:
  One of the key components of predictive analytics is **behavioral analysis**, where AI systems monitor normal network activity to establish a baseline. When deviations from this baseline occur—such as unusual login times, unexpected file access, or abnormal traffic patterns—AI systems can flag these activities as potentially malicious. For example, an AI system could detect an insider threat by identifying anomalous data access patterns before any data is exfiltrated.

- **Attack Pattern Recognition**:
  AI systems trained on historical cyberattacks can recognize the early stages of **malware deployment, DDoS attacks**, or **phishing campaigns**. By identifying the **tactics, techniques, and procedures (TTPs)** used by attackers, AI can anticipate the **next steps** in an attack and recommend defensive measures. This allows cybersecurity teams to proactively address vulnerabilities and adjust defenses based on the predicted behavior of attackers.

2. Proactive Defense Strategies Using Predictive Analytics

By integrating predictive analytics into their cybersecurity strategies, organizations can shift from **reactive** to **proactive** defense models. This proactive approach aligns with **guerrilla tactics** by emphasizing the importance of **anticipating the enemy's movements** and preparing defenses in advance.

- **Preemptive Patching and Vulnerability Management**:
  AI-powered predictive analytics can identify which systems or software are most likely to be targeted based on current **threat intelligence**. By analyzing known vulnerabilities and attacker activity, AI can recommend **preemptive patching** of critical systems, preventing attackers from exploiting weaknesses before they become active targets.
- **Dynamic Network Reconfiguration**:
  Predictive analytics can be integrated with **Software Defined Networking (SDN)** to allow for **dynamic network reconfiguration** in response to emerging threats. If AI predicts an attack on a particular segment of the network, SDN can automatically adjust network paths, reroute traffic, or isolate vulnerable systems, making it more difficult for attackers to penetrate defenses.

Case Study: Financial Institution Prevents APT Using Predictive Analytics

A large financial institution successfully used **predictive analytics** to prevent an **Advanced Persistent Threat (APT)** targeting its internal systems. The AI-driven system identified **suspicious lateral movement** within the network by an insider threat that had been compromised through a phishing attack. The predictive analytics platform flagged the anomalous behavior early, allowing the security team to isolate the compromised system and prevent the APT from accessing sensitive financial data.

By leveraging **AI-powered predictive analytics**, the institution implemented **proactive defenses** that disrupted the attacker's campaign before significant damage could occur, demonstrating how **anticipatory action** is a critical component of modern cyber defense.

Cybersecurity Implications of 5G Networks and IoT Devices

The rollout of **5G networks** and the proliferation of **Internet of Things (IoT) devices** are transforming industries, from **smart cities** and **connected vehicles** to **industrial automation** and **smart healthcare**. While these technologies offer significant benefits, they also introduce new cybersecurity challenges due to the **increased attack surface**, the **decentralized nature of devices**, and the **speed** at which data is transferred.

1. The Security Risks of 5G Networks

The shift to **5G networks** is a double-edged sword for cybersecurity. While 5G offers **faster data transfer rates** and **lower latency**, it also increases the number of **entry points** for attackers due to the **decentralized** architecture and the large number of **connected devices**. Traditional perimeter-based security models are no longer effective in this environment, requiring a shift to **dynamic, distributed defense strategies**.

- **Edge Computing and Decentralized Security:**
  5G networks rely on **edge computing**, where data is processed closer to the source rather than in centralized data centers. While this reduces latency, it also means that data is more vulnerable as it traverses between **edge nodes**. Attackers can exploit weak points in edge devices, leading to data breaches or denial-of-service attacks. Security teams must adopt **decentralized security models**, where **zero trust architecture** and **endpoint protection** are deployed across the network's edge.
- **Increased Attack Surface:**
  The increase in **connected devices** within 5G networks, particularly in **smart cities** and **critical infrastructure**, means that each device becomes a potential attack vector. This dramatically increases the **attack surface**, making it harder to defend against threats. AI-driven systems are crucial for **monitoring** and **securing** these vast networks in real-time.

2. The Challenges of Securing IoT Devices

IoT devices are particularly vulnerable to cyberattacks due to their **limited security features** and **lack of regular updates**. Many IoT devices are designed with **convenience** in mind rather than security, and they are often deployed in **critical sectors** such as **healthcare, transportation,** and **manufacturing.**

- **IoT Botnets:**
  One of the most prominent threats posed by IoT devices is the creation of **botnets**, where compromised IoT devices are used to launch **DDoS attacks** or other malicious activities. For example, the **Mirai botnet** leveraged unsecured IoT devices to launch massive DDoS attacks, highlighting the need for improved **device security** and **network segmentation**.
- **Device Authentication and Encryption:**
  Securing IoT devices requires the implementation of **strong authentication protocols** and **encryption** to protect data as it

travels between devices and the cloud. AI-driven systems can play a key role in monitoring IoT devices for signs of compromise, automatically quarantining or updating devices when vulnerabilities are detected.

Case Study: Securing Smart City Infrastructure with AI and SDN

A major **smart city initiative** leveraged **AI** and **SDN** to secure its **IoT infrastructure**. The city deployed millions of IoT devices to manage traffic systems, utilities, and public safety. To defend against potential cyberattacks, the city's cybersecurity team implemented **AI-driven threat detection** to monitor IoT traffic in real-time, combined with **SDN** to dynamically segment the network and isolate compromised devices.

By continuously analyzing traffic patterns and device behavior, AI was able to detect anomalous activity indicative of botnet formation. **SDN** allowed the team to **quarantine** infected devices and reroute critical traffic, ensuring that essential services remained operational while threats were mitigated.

Cloud Security: Leveraging AI and Blockchain for Enhanced Protection

As more organizations migrate to the **cloud**, ensuring the security of **cloud environments** becomes paramount. The **distributed nature** of cloud infrastructure introduces challenges related to **data privacy**, **access control**, and **compliance**. However, emerging technologies such as **AI** and **blockchain** can be leveraged to enhance cloud security, creating a **resilient, decentralized defense** that aligns with **guerrilla warfare tactics**.

1. The Role of AI in Cloud Security

AI is increasingly being used to enhance **cloud security** by providing **real-time monitoring**, **automated threat detection**, and **incident response**. AI systems can analyze large volumes of data generated by cloud environments, identifying anomalies and threats before they cause harm.

- **AI-Driven Access Control**:
  In cloud environments, **access control** is a critical security measure. AI-driven systems can continuously monitor user access patterns, automatically adjusting **permissions** based on user behavior and the sensitivity of the data being accessed. This reduces the risk of **insider threats** and ensures that only authorized users have access to critical data.
- **Automated Threat Detection and Response**:
  AI-driven cloud security systems can detect **unauthorized access attempts**, **misconfigurations**, and **malicious activity** in real-time. When a threat is detected, AI can automatically trigger **security protocols**, such as revoking access, isolating compromised virtual machines, or blocking malicious IP addresses.

2. Blockchain for Decentralized Cloud Security

Blockchain technology offers a decentralized approach to securing cloud environments, making it an ideal tool for organizations that need to protect sensitive data from tampering, unauthorized access, or data breaches. By leveraging blockchain's inherent immutability and **distributed consensus**, organizations can create **tamper-proof** records of data access and transactions.

- **Blockchain for Secure Identity Management**:
  Blockchain can be used to create **secure identity management systems** in cloud environments. Each user's identity can be cryptographically linked to a blockchain, ensuring that **authentication records** are tamper-proof and auditable. This eliminates the risk of **credential theft** and **man-in-the-middle attacks**.

- **Decentralized Data Storage and Integrity:**
  Blockchain can be used to ensure the **integrity** of data stored in the cloud. By distributing data across multiple blockchain nodes and verifying its integrity through **cryptographic hashes**, organizations can ensure that their data has not been altered or corrupted. This is particularly useful for industries that require **data immutability**, such as healthcare or financial services.

Case Study: Blockchain-Enhanced Cloud Security in Healthcare

A leading **healthcare provider** integrated **blockchain technology** into its **cloud security infrastructure** to protect sensitive patient data. By using blockchain to secure **patient records** and **identity management systems**, the organization was able to ensure that all access to patient data was **auditable** and **tamper-proof**. In addition, **AI-driven threat detection** monitored cloud activity, automatically flagging unauthorized access attempts and isolating compromised accounts.

The combination of **AI** and **blockchain** created a **resilient defense** that protected patient data from cyberattacks while ensuring compliance with **data privacy regulations** such as **HIPAA**.

The Role of Autonomous Systems in Cyber Warfare

Autonomous systems are becoming increasingly important in the realm of **cyber warfare**, as both attackers and defenders look to **automate** their operations. Autonomous systems, powered by AI, can detect, analyze, and respond to cyber threats at **machine speed**, outpacing human adversaries. In the future, **autonomous cyber defense systems** will become essential for defending against the growing scale and complexity of cyberattacks.

1. AI-Driven Autonomous Cyber Defense

AI-driven autonomous systems are capable of detecting and responding to cyber threats without the need for human intervention. These systems use **machine learning** to continuously learn from new attack patterns and improve their defensive capabilities over time.

- **Autonomous Incident Response:**
  Autonomous systems can automatically respond to cyber incidents by isolating compromised systems, blocking malicious traffic, and initiating recovery processes. This allows defenders to **contain** threats in real-time, minimizing the damage caused by cyberattacks. For example, an autonomous system could detect a ransomware attack in progress, automatically **encrypt backup data**, and initiate **disaster recovery** protocols to restore systems.
- **Adaptive Learning for Cyber Defense:**
  Autonomous systems use **adaptive learning algorithms** to evolve their defense strategies based on the behavior of attackers. This allows them to continuously improve their ability to defend against **advanced persistent threats (APTs)** and **zero-day attacks**. Autonomous systems can also simulate attack scenarios, testing their defenses and identifying vulnerabilities before attackers can exploit them.

2. The Role of Autonomous Systems in Offensive Cyber Operations

While autonomous systems are primarily used for defense, they also have a role to play in **offensive cyber operations**. Autonomous systems can be deployed to identify and exploit vulnerabilities in enemy networks, disable adversary infrastructure, or launch **automated counterattacks** against attackers.

- **Automated Counterattacks:**
  In the future, autonomous systems may be used to launch **automated counterattacks** against cyber adversaries. For example, an autonomous system could identify the **command-and-control (C2) servers** used by an attacker and

deploy a **countermeasure** to disable the server, disrupting the attacker's operations. These systems could also be used to **exfiltrate intelligence** from adversary networks, providing valuable insights into their attack strategies.
- **Cyber Guerrilla Tactics with Autonomous Systems**: Autonomous systems can be integrated into **cyber guerrilla tactics**, using **hit-and-run strategies** to disrupt larger, more powerful adversaries. For example, autonomous systems could deploy **decoy networks** or **honeypots** to confuse attackers and waste their resources. These systems could then launch targeted counterattacks, exploiting vulnerabilities in the attacker's infrastructure.

Case Study: Autonomous Cyber Defense at a Major Financial Institution

A major financial institution deployed **autonomous cyber defense systems** to protect its global network from **nation-state attackers**. The autonomous systems continuously monitored network activity, using **machine learning** to detect new attack vectors. When a threat was detected, the system automatically **quarantined** the compromised network segment, blocked malicious IP addresses, and launched a **counterattack** to disable the attacker's command-and-control servers.

By leveraging **autonomous systems**, the financial institution was able to defend against nation-state-level attacks while minimizing the need for human intervention. The autonomous system's ability to **learn** from each attack improved its defenses over time, ensuring that the institution stayed ahead of evolving threats.

Conclusion: The Future of Cyber Defense Through Emerging Technologies

The integration of **emerging technologies** such as **predictive analytics, 5G networks, IoT devices, cloud security,** and **autonomous systems** into **cyber guerrilla warfare tactics** will be essential for defending against **next-generation threats**. By adopting **proactive defense strategies** that leverage **AI-driven predictive analytics**, organizations can anticipate and neutralize threats before they escalate. As **5G** and **IoT** expand the attack surface, defenders must adopt **dynamic defense models** that incorporate **AI, SDN,** and **zero trust principles** to secure their networks.

Cloud security will require the integration of **AI** and **blockchain** to protect distributed environments, while **autonomous systems** will play a key role in automating cyber defense and offense. As attackers become more sophisticated, defenders must continuously adapt their strategies, leveraging the full potential of emerging technologies to stay one step ahead.

By integrating these technologies into **cyber guerrilla warfare tactics**, organizations can create **adaptive, resilient,** and **proactive defenses** that effectively counter the evolving cyber threat landscape.

Chapter 21: Preparing for the Future: Next-Generation Cyber Defense

Introduction

The future of cybersecurity is rapidly evolving, driven by **emerging technologies** like **quantum computing,** the **Internet of Things (IoT), artificial intelligence (AI),** and **automation**. These advancements are transforming the way we live and work, but they are also introducing new and unprecedented challenges to cyber defense. **Cyber threats** are growing in complexity, with attackers leveraging increasingly sophisticated tools and techniques to exploit vulnerabilities in next-generation systems. As these technologies advance, defenders must stay **one step ahead**, constantly adapting their strategies and tactics to confront evolving threats.

The introduction of **quantum computing** will have a profound impact on both the **offensive** and **defensive** capabilities of cyber actors, enabling quantum-enabled attackers to break traditional cryptographic systems. Similarly, the proliferation of **IoT devices** will greatly expand the attack surface for malicious actors, making it imperative to develop **next-generation cyber defense strategies** that account for these changes.

In this chapter, we will explore how emerging technologies like **quantum computing** and **IoT** will impact cyber defense, how **guerrilla tactics** will evolve to address new threats, and how **AI, SDN,** and **automation** will continue to play a pivotal role in shaping the future of **cyber warfare**. We will also emphasize the importance of **continuous adaptation**, ensuring that cyber defenders can stay ahead of attackers in an ever-changing threat environment.

How Emerging Technologies Like Quantum Computing and IoT Will Impact Cyber Defense

Emerging technologies like **quantum computing** and the **Internet of Things (IoT)** have the potential to fundamentally reshape the cybersecurity landscape. While these innovations offer significant benefits to society, they also introduce new vulnerabilities that cyber defenders must address.

1. QUANTUM COMPUTING: A DOUBLE-EDGED SWORD

Quantum computing represents one of the most transformative technologies on the horizon. With its ability to solve complex mathematical problems far more quickly than classical computers, quantum computing promises breakthroughs in fields such as **drug discovery**, **materials science**, and **cryptography**. However, it also poses a significant threat to current cybersecurity defenses.

THE THREAT TO CRYPTOGRAPHY

Quantum computers will have the ability to break widely used encryption algorithms, such as **RSA** and **ECC** (Elliptic Curve Cryptography), which underpin the security of most modern communication systems. This means that encrypted data, once considered secure, will be vulnerable to decryption by quantum-enabled attackers.

- **Quantum-Safe Cryptography**:
  To address the threat posed by quantum computing, cybersecurity experts are working on developing **quantum-safe cryptographic algorithms**. These **post-quantum cryptographic** methods are designed to withstand attacks from quantum computers, ensuring that sensitive information remains protected even in a quantum-enabled world. Organizations will need to transition to these quantum-safe methods before large-scale quantum computing becomes a reality.
- **Quantum Encryption**:
  On the defensive side, quantum computing also holds the promise of enabling **quantum encryption** methods, such as **Quantum Key Distribution (QKD)**. QKD allows for the secure exchange of encryption keys by leveraging the principles of quantum mechanics. Any attempt to intercept the key would disturb the quantum state of the particles involved, alerting the parties to the presence of an eavesdropper. This could pave the way for **unbreakable encryption**, offering a countermeasure to the quantum decryption threat.

THE QUANTUM ARMS RACE

The development of quantum computing is likely to spark a **cyber arms race** between nation-states and major corporations. As quantum computers become more capable, attackers will seek to leverage them for cyberattacks, while defenders will race to implement **quantum-safe solutions**. Cyber defense teams must remain vigilant and prepare for the possibility of **quantum-enabled attacks** by staying informed about advances in **quantum cryptography** and investing in quantum-resistant technologies.

2. THE INTERNET OF THINGS (IOT): EXPANDING THE ATTACK SURFACE

The widespread adoption of **IoT devices** is revolutionizing industries, enabling smart cities, connected vehicles, and industrial automation. However, the proliferation of IoT devices also introduces significant cybersecurity challenges, as these devices often lack robust security measures and are connected to critical networks.

INCREASED ATTACK VECTORS

IoT devices—ranging from **smart thermostats** and **wearables** to **industrial sensors** and **connected cars**—create an expansive and **distributed attack surface**. Many of these devices are not designed with security in mind and may be vulnerable to basic attacks such as **DDoS** or **botnet hijacking**. Compromised IoT devices can be used as entry points into more secure networks or as part of larger attack campaigns.

- **IoT Botnets**:
  Attackers have already demonstrated their ability to harness IoT devices for large-scale **botnet attacks**, such as the infamous **Mirai botnet**, which used infected IoT devices to launch massive DDoS attacks. As more IoT devices come online, the threat posed by **IoT botnets** will continue to grow, making it imperative for defenders to develop strategies for detecting and mitigating IoT-based attacks.

SECURING THE IOT ECOSYSTEM

To address the cybersecurity risks associated with IoT devices, defenders must focus on **securing the IoT ecosystem** by implementing strong **authentication mechanisms, encryption,** and **device management** protocols.

- **Zero Trust Architecture for IoT**:
  The **Zero Trust** model will play a critical role in securing IoT environments. By adopting **Zero Trust** principles, organizations can ensure that **every IoT device** connected to the network is continuously authenticated and authorized, preventing unauthorized access and minimizing the risk of lateral movement by attackers.
- **IoT Device Management**:
  Proper **device management** is essential for maintaining the security of IoT devices. This includes regular **firmware updates, vulnerability assessments,** and **patch management**. AI-driven systems can help automate the detection of vulnerabilities in IoT devices, ensuring that they are secured before attackers can exploit them.

As IoT continues to expand, the need for **strong IoT security** practices will become even more pressing. Organizations must prepare for the security challenges posed by billions of interconnected devices, many of which may be vulnerable to exploitation.

Evolving Guerrilla Tactics for New Threats

As new technologies like **quantum computing** and **IoT** emerge, **cyber guerrilla warfare tactics** must evolve to address the changing threat landscape. **Guerrilla-style tactics** rely on **mobility, deception,** and **asymmetry** to defend against larger, better-resourced adversaries. In the face of next-generation threats, these tactics will need to adapt to leverage new technologies and exploit emerging vulnerabilities.

1. ASYMMETRIC DEFENSE IN A QUANTUM-ENABLED WORLD

In the context of **quantum-enabled threats**, **asymmetric defense tactics** will become even more critical for organizations seeking to defend against **nation-state adversaries** and **well-funded attackers** who may possess quantum capabilities.

- **Decentralized Cryptographic Systems**:
  One potential **guerrilla tactic** in a quantum-enabled world is the use of **decentralized cryptographic systems** that rely on distributed consensus mechanisms, such as **blockchain**, to secure communications and transactions. By decentralizing cryptographic infrastructure, organizations can reduce their reliance on single points of failure, making it more difficult for quantum-enabled attackers to compromise their systems.
- **Quantum Deception**:
  Deception tactics will also evolve in the quantum era. For example, defenders could deploy **quantum decoys** or **quantum honeypots** to lure quantum attackers into wasting computational resources on false targets. These decoys could be designed to appear as high-value cryptographic keys or sensitive data, tricking attackers into expending time and effort while the real assets remain secure.

2. DYNAMIC DEFENSE FOR IOT ENVIRONMENTS

The **distributed nature** of IoT environments calls for **dynamic defense tactics** that can rapidly adapt to new threats. **Guerrilla warfare tactics** will need to leverage **real-time threat intelligence** and **AI-driven automation** to stay ahead of attackers targeting IoT devices.

- **Hit-and-Run Tactics for IoT Defense**:
  In an IoT environment, defenders can apply **hit-and-run**

tactics by constantly shifting the network configuration and security protocols of connected devices. For example, defenders could periodically **rotate encryption keys**, **change access control policies**, and **reroute network traffic** to confuse attackers and limit their ability to gain a foothold. These tactics make it difficult for attackers to sustain long-term attacks against IoT networks.

- **Attrition Warfare with AI-Driven Response:**
  AI-driven attrition warfare can be used to exhaust attackers targeting IoT environments. By automating **incident response** and deploying **decoy IoT devices**, defenders can overwhelm attackers with false leads and continuously disrupt their operations. This forces attackers to expend resources chasing decoys while the real systems remain secure.

As the threat landscape continues to evolve, **cyber guerrilla warfare tactics** will need to adapt, using **asymmetry**, **deception**, and **mobility** to defend against quantum-enabled attackers and IoT-based threats.

THE FUTURE ROLE OF AI, SDN, AND AUTOMATION IN CYBER WARFARE

Artificial Intelligence (AI), **Software Defined Networking (SDN)**, and **automation** are already transforming **cyber defense**, but their role will become even more pivotal as new threats emerge. These technologies will be key enablers of **next-generation cyber warfare**, allowing defenders to respond to attacks in **real-time**, automate **threat detection**, and dynamically reconfigure networks to prevent breaches.

1. AI AS A CENTRAL PLAYER IN CYBER DEFENSE

AI will continue to be a **central player** in **cyber defense**, with its ability to **predict attacks, analyze massive data sets**, and **respond autonomously** to threats. AI-driven systems will become increasingly self-learning, allowing them to detect **previously unknown threats** and **evolve** alongside the tactics used by cyber adversaries.

- **AI for Real-Time Threat Intelligence**:
  In the future, AI systems will serve as the **nervous system** of cybersecurity, continuously collecting and analyzing data from **global threat intelligence networks**. These systems will provide **real-time insights** into emerging threats, allowing defenders to proactively adjust their defenses based on the latest attack trends.
- **Autonomous Cyber Defense**:
  AI will play a critical role in enabling **autonomous cyber defense**, where systems can detect, respond to, and mitigate threats without human intervention. These AI-driven defense systems will use **machine learning models** to continuously refine their strategies, ensuring that they remain effective against **advanced persistent threats (APTs)** and **nation-state actors**.

2. SDN FOR DYNAMIC, SELF-HEALING NETWORKS

As cyber threats become more dynamic, the need for **real-time network reconfiguration** will grow. **Software Defined Networking (SDN)** will enable the creation of **self-healing networks** that can automatically adjust their configuration in response to detected threats, ensuring that the network remains operational even during an attack.

- **AI-SDN Integration for Dynamic Defense**:
  The integration of **AI** with **SDN** will allow organizations to create **dynamic defense environments** that can automatically **segment** and **reroute traffic** in response to attacks. This will be particularly important in defending **critical infrastructure** and **IoT environments**, where attackers may attempt to disrupt operations by targeting specific network components.

- **Zero-Trust Networks with SDN:**
  Zero-trust architectures will be enhanced by **SDN**, allowing defenders to continuously verify the identity and integrity of users, devices, and data flows. With **AI-driven access control**, SDN-enabled networks can automatically enforce **granular security policies**, ensuring that only authorized entities have access to sensitive systems.

3. AUTOMATION IN INCIDENT RESPONSE

As cyberattacks grow in **speed** and **sophistication**, the role of **automation** in incident response will become more critical. **Automated incident response systems** will enable defenders to quickly **detect, contain,** and **neutralize threats** before they can cause significant damage.

- **AI-Driven Playbooks for Automated Response:**
  AI-driven **automation playbooks** will allow defenders to predefine **response workflows** for specific types of cyber incidents. When a threat is detected, the system can automatically execute a series of actions, such as **quarantining infected systems, blocking malicious IP addresses,** and **alerting the security team**. These automated responses will drastically reduce the time between detection and mitigation, limiting the impact of cyberattacks.
- **Self-Learning Defense Systems:**
  Future defense systems will leverage **self-learning capabilities**, allowing them to continuously **improve** their response tactics based on new attack patterns. These systems will learn from past incidents, refining their strategies to ensure they are always prepared for the latest threats.

The future of **AI, SDN,** and **automation** in cyber warfare will be defined by their ability to create **dynamic, self-healing defenses** that adapt in real-time to evolving threats. These technologies will be essential for defending against increasingly sophisticated cyber adversaries.

Continuous Adaptation: Staying Ahead of Attackers in an Ever-Changing Environment

One of the most important principles in **next-generation cyber defense** is the need for **continuous adaptation**. The cyber threat landscape is constantly evolving, with attackers developing new techniques and exploiting emerging technologies. To stay ahead of these threats, defenders must adopt a mindset of **continuous improvement**, ensuring that their defenses evolve as quickly as the attacks they face.

1. Adaptive Defense Strategies

To stay ahead of attackers, organizations must implement **adaptive defense strategies** that can adjust in real-time based on the latest threat intelligence. **AI, automation**, and **SDN** will play a crucial role in enabling this adaptability, allowing defenders to quickly reconfigure their defenses in response to new threats.

- **Real-Time Threat Modeling**:
  AI-driven threat modeling will allow organizations to simulate potential attack scenarios based on current threat intelligence. By continuously updating these models, defenders can identify **weak points** in their defenses and proactively address vulnerabilities before they are exploited.
- **Dynamic Security Policies**:
  Future cybersecurity systems will use **dynamic security policies** that can be adjusted in real-time based on the current threat landscape. For example, if a new vulnerability is discovered in a widely used software platform, AI systems can automatically update security policies to block traffic to and from vulnerable systems until a patch is applied.

2. CONTINUOUS LEARNING AND INNOVATION

Cyber defense teams must embrace a culture of **continuous learning** and **innovation** to stay ahead of attackers. This means regularly **updating defense technologies**, participating in **cyber exercises**, and staying informed about the latest developments in the cybersecurity field.

- **Cybersecurity Training and Exercises**:
  Regular **cybersecurity exercises**, such as **red team/blue team simulations**, will be essential for preparing defenders to face new threats. These exercises allow organizations to test their defenses in realistic attack scenarios, identifying areas for improvement and refining their response strategies.
- **Collaboration and Intelligence Sharing**:
  Collaboration between organizations, governments, and international partners will be key to staying ahead of cyber threats. By sharing **threat intelligence** and **best practices**, defenders can improve their understanding of emerging attack techniques and develop coordinated strategies to mitigate them.

3. THE ROLE OF AI IN CONTINUOUS ADAPTATION

AI will be a **driving force** behind **continuous adaptation** in cyber defense. As AI systems become more **self-learning** and **autonomous**, they will be able to continuously **evolve** their defenses in response to new threats. AI-driven defense systems will monitor the threat landscape in real-time, adapting their strategies to ensure they remain effective against the latest attack vectors.

- **Self-Healing AI Systems**:
  In the future, AI systems will be capable of **self-healing**, automatically repairing vulnerabilities and reconfiguring defenses in response to attacks. This continuous adaptation will enable organizations to maintain a **resilient defense posture**, even in the face of rapidly evolving threats.

By embracing **continuous adaptation**, defenders can stay ahead of attackers, ensuring that their cybersecurity systems remain effective in an ever-changing threat environment.

Conclusion: Preparing for the Future of Cyber Defense

The future of **cyber defense** will be defined by the ability to **adapt** to emerging technologies and evolving threats. As **quantum computing, IoT**, and **AI** reshape the cyber landscape, defenders must be prepared to face new challenges while leveraging the power of **AI, SDN**, and **automation** to create **dynamic, self-healing defenses**.

Guerrilla warfare tactics will continue to play a critical role in defending against larger, more powerful adversaries, with **asymmetric strategies, deception**, and **attrition warfare** evolving to address next-generation threats. At the same time, **continuous adaptation** will be essential for staying ahead of attackers in an ever-changing environment.

By preparing for the future, adopting **next-generation technologies**, and maintaining a mindset of **continuous improvement**, organizations can ensure that they are ready to defend against the sophisticated cyber threats of tomorrow.

CONCLUSION: THE GUERRILLA DEFENDER'S PATH

Introduction

The modern cybersecurity battlefield is an unforgiving environment where traditional defenses are no longer sufficient to withstand sophisticated and well-resourced attackers. Nation-states, organized crime syndicates, and advanced persistent threats (APTs) are continuously evolving their methods, employing techniques that are increasingly complex, stealthy, and adaptable. To defend against these adversaries, cybersecurity teams must adopt a **guerrilla-style approach**—one that emphasizes **agility, deception, proactivity,** and **unpredictability.**

The **guerrilla defender** draws inspiration from the principles of asymmetric warfare, utilizing **hit-and-run tactics, dynamic defenses,** and **deception strategies** to outmaneuver and exhaust attackers. By leveraging cutting-edge technologies such as **Artificial Intelligence (AI), Software Defined Networking (SDN),** and **automation,** defenders can create flexible, adaptive systems that can respond to threats in real-time while maintaining operational resilience.

This concluding chapter will distill the key lessons of **cyber guerrilla warfare,** offering practical takeaways for implementing these tactics in real-world cyber defense. We will also explore how organizations can build an **adaptive, agile,** and **resilient** cyber defense strategy that leverages the power of technology and tactics to stay one step ahead of attackers. Finally, we will underscore the importance of maintaining a **proactive** and **unpredictable** defense posture, ensuring that cyber defenders remain agile in an ever-changing threat landscape.

Key Takeaways for Implementing Guerrilla Tactics in Cyber Defense

The principles of **guerrilla warfare** provide a powerful framework for defending against larger, better-funded, and more technically advanced adversaries. The **guerrilla defender** relies on **asymmetry, mobility, deception,** and **attrition** to continuously disrupt and outmaneuver attackers. Below are the key takeaways for implementing these guerrilla tactics in modern cyber defense.

1. LEVERAGE ASYMMETRIC DEFENSE TO OUTMANEUVER ADVERSARIES

In traditional guerrilla warfare, small, agile forces exploit the vulnerabilities of a larger enemy. This principle translates directly into cyber defense, where defenders often face attackers with more resources and technical expertise. The key to success lies in **asymmetric defense**—using strategies that maximize the defender's strengths while targeting the attacker's weaknesses.

- **Exploit Vulnerabilities in Attacker Infrastructure**:
  Guerrilla defenders should seek to exploit **weak points** in the attacker's infrastructure. This could involve identifying **command-and-control (C2) servers, communication channels**, or **malware distribution networks** that can be disrupted or neutralized. By forcing attackers to defend their own infrastructure, defenders can shift the balance of power in their favor.
- **Utilize Decoy Systems and Honeypots**:
  Deception plays a central role in asymmetric defense. By deploying **honeypots, honeynets**, and other decoy systems, defenders can lure attackers into wasting time and resources on **false targets**. These decoys provide valuable intelligence on the attacker's tactics, techniques, and procedures (TTPs) while keeping critical systems secure.

2. APPLY HIT-AND-RUN TACTICS FOR RAPID RESPONSE AND CONTAINMENT

Hit-and-run tactics are a core component of guerrilla warfare, enabling defenders to strike quickly, inflict damage, and retreat before the enemy can respond. In the context of cyber defense, these tactics involve **rapid detection, containment**, and **response** to threats before they can spread or cause significant damage.

- **Rapid Isolation and Segmentation**:
  When a breach is detected, the defender's priority should be to **isolate the affected systems** as quickly as possible. Using SDN, defenders can create **dynamic network segments** to

quarantine compromised devices, preventing lateral movement by the attacker. This minimizes the impact of the breach while allowing the security team to investigate and mitigate the threat.
- **Hit-and-Run Counterattacks**:
In some cases, guerrilla defenders may choose to launch **preemptive strikes** or **counterattacks** against attacker infrastructure. This could involve exploiting vulnerabilities in the attacker's tools or infrastructure to disrupt their operations. By quickly engaging and then retreating, defenders can keep attackers off-balance, forcing them to divert resources and attention away from the primary target.

3. USE ATTRITION WARFARE TO EXHAUST ATTACKERS

A hallmark of guerrilla warfare is **attrition**—the process of wearing down an adversary over time. In the cyber domain, attrition warfare involves continually **disrupting** and **frustrating** attackers, forcing them to expend time, resources, and effort without achieving their objectives.

- **Automated Deception and Response**:
AI-driven deception tactics can play a key role in attrition warfare. By deploying **automated defenses** that generate false data, redirect attackers to decoy systems, and continuously change the network landscape, defenders can create an environment where attackers are constantly on the defensive. Over time, this forces attackers to waste resources while the real systems remain secure.
- **Delay and Disrupt Attacker Operations**:
Guerrilla defenders should aim to **delay** and **disrupt** attackers at every stage of the kill chain. This might involve deploying **traffic obfuscation** techniques, **rotating encryption keys**, or changing access control policies in real-time. By creating obstacles at every turn, defenders can slow down attackers, reducing their effectiveness and increasing the likelihood that they will abandon the attack.

How to Build an Adaptive, Agile, and Resilient Cyber Defense Strategy

In a world where cyber threats are constantly evolving, building a **cyber defense strategy** that is **adaptive**, **agile**, and **resilient** is critical for long-term success. The guerrilla defender's strength lies in their ability to rapidly adapt to new threats, recover from attacks, and remain agile in the face of uncertainty.

1. Adaptive Defense Through Continuous Learning

The cornerstone of an adaptive defense is the ability to **learn continuously** from both successful and unsuccessful attacks. By leveraging **AI** and **machine learning** technologies, organizations can create **self-learning defense systems** that analyze threat data in real-time, identifying patterns and emerging trends that human analysts may miss.

- **AI-Driven Threat Intelligence**:
  AI systems can continuously collect and analyze **threat intelligence** from a wide range of sources, including internal network logs, global threat feeds, and open-source data. This enables defenders to stay ahead of attackers by identifying new vulnerabilities and attack vectors before they can be exploited.
- **Proactive Defense Adjustments**:
  Adaptive defense systems should be capable of making **proactive adjustments** based on real-time threat intelligence. For example, AI-driven **predictive analytics** can identify **high-risk systems** or users that are likely to be targeted, allowing defenders to implement additional safeguards in advance. By staying proactive, defenders can reduce the attack surface and prevent breaches before they occur.

2. AGILITY IN CYBER DEFENSE: RAPID RESPONSE AND FLEXIBILITY

Agility is essential in cyber defense, as attackers often strike without warning and can rapidly change their tactics. An agile defense strategy enables organizations to respond quickly to new threats and adapt their defenses in real-time.

- **Dynamic Network Segmentation with SDN:**
  One of the key technologies that supports agility in cyber defense is **Software Defined Networking (SDN)**. SDN allows defenders to **dynamically reconfigure** the network based on real-time threat intelligence. For example, if an attacker is attempting to move laterally through the network, SDN can automatically create new network segments to isolate compromised systems and prevent further spread.
- **Automation for Rapid Incident Response:**
  Automation is critical for achieving agility in incident response. By deploying **AI-driven automation playbooks**, defenders can respond to incidents within seconds, executing predefined workflows that include isolating affected systems, blocking malicious traffic, and notifying the security team. This rapid response minimizes the time attackers have to exploit vulnerabilities, reducing the overall impact of the breach.

3. BUILDING RESILIENCE AGAINST FUTURE ATTACKS

A **resilient cyber defense strategy** is one that not only defends against current threats but also prepares for future attacks. Resilience involves creating systems that can **withstand attacks**, **recover quickly**, and continue to operate even under adverse conditions.

- **Redundancy and Failover Systems:**
  Resilience can be achieved through the implementation of **redundant systems** and **failover mechanisms**. These systems ensure that if one part of the network is compromised, other

parts can take over, maintaining operational continuity. For example, critical data and services can be mirrored across multiple servers, with automatic failover systems in place to redirect traffic in the event of a breach.
- **Resilient AI-Driven Security Operations Centers (SOCs)**: The future of resilient cyber defense will likely involve **AI-driven SOCs** that can automatically detect and respond to threats across a distributed environment. These SOCs will have the capability to dynamically adapt to new threats, using **self-healing networks** and **AI-powered forensics** to investigate and recover from attacks quickly.

THE IMPORTANCE OF STAYING PROACTIVE AND UNPREDICTABLE

The key to success in **guerrilla warfare** is **proactivity** and **unpredictability**. In the cyber realm, this means staying ahead of attackers by adopting a **proactive defense posture** and maintaining an element of **surprise** that confounds adversaries and keeps them guessing.

1. PROACTIVE THREAT HUNTING AND MITIGATION

Proactive threat hunting involves searching for potential vulnerabilities and indicators of compromise before an attacker has the opportunity to exploit them. This shift from a reactive to a proactive mindset is essential for modern cyber defense.

- **AI-Enhanced Threat Hunting**:
  Using **AI-enhanced threat hunting** tools, cybersecurity teams can continuously scan their networks for suspicious activity or weak points that could be exploited by attackers. AI-driven tools can correlate data from a variety of sources to identify subtle indicators of compromise, allowing defenders to **mitigate threats** before they evolve into full-scale breaches.

- **Vulnerability Management and Patch Automation**:
  Proactive defenders must also focus on **vulnerability management**, ensuring that known vulnerabilities are patched before they can be exploited. **AI-driven automation** can streamline this process by continuously scanning for missing patches, prioritizing vulnerabilities based on risk, and automatically applying updates across the network.

2. THE POWER OF UNPREDICTABILITY IN CYBER DEFENSE

Unpredictability is one of the most powerful tools in the guerrilla defender's arsenal. By constantly changing the **defensive landscape**, defenders can create an environment where attackers are unsure of their next move, making it difficult for them to establish a foothold or execute their plans.

- **Dynamic Defense Systems**:
  Dynamic defense systems leverage **SDN** and **AI** to continually shift the network environment, changing **IP addresses**, **access control policies**, and **traffic routing** in real-time. These constant changes force attackers to continually reassess their strategies, increasing the likelihood that they will make mistakes or abandon their efforts altogether.
- **Unpredictable Incident Response**:
  Another key aspect of unpredictability is ensuring that **incident response procedures** are not predictable or formulaic. By varying response tactics and strategies, defenders can keep attackers off-balance. For example, defenders might use a combination of **decoy systems**, **traffic rerouting**, and **honeypots** to create confusion, preventing attackers from accurately assessing the effectiveness of their attacks.

Conclusion: Embracing the Guerrilla Defender's Path

The **guerrilla defender's path** offers a new approach to **cyber defense**, one that emphasizes **agility**, **adaptability**, and **asymmetry** to overcome even the most formidable adversaries. By leveraging the power of **AI**, **SDN**, **automation**, and **cyber guerrilla warfare tactics**, defenders can create **dynamic, resilient,** and **proactive defenses** capable of responding to the ever-evolving cyber threat landscape.

The key lessons of the **guerrilla defender** can be summarized as follows:

- **Leverage asymmetric tactics** to outmaneuver attackers, exploiting their vulnerabilities while protecting your most valuable assets.
- **Stay proactive** by adopting AI-driven threat intelligence and continuously hunting for potential vulnerabilities before they can be exploited.
- **Embrace unpredictability** by deploying dynamic defenses that change the attack surface in real-time, preventing attackers from gaining a foothold.
- **Focus on agility and resilience** by building systems that can adapt to new threats and recover quickly from attacks, ensuring operational continuity in the face of adversity.

By embracing these principles, the **guerrilla defender** can successfully navigate the challenges of modern cyber warfare, maintaining a **proactive** and **unpredictable defense posture** that keeps attackers on the defensive and protects critical assets from harm.

As we look to the future, it is clear that the **guerrilla defender's path** will continue to be a valuable strategy in the ongoing battle for **cybersecurity**. By staying agile, adaptable, and resilient, cyber defenders can remain one step ahead of their adversaries, ensuring that they are prepared for whatever challenges lie ahead.